Camping Guideposts

Camping Guideposts

Handbook for Counselors

by
LLOYD D. MATTSON

MOODY PRESS
CHICAGO

© 1972, by
THE MOODY BIBLE INSTITUTE
OF CHICAGO

ISBN: 0-8024-1150-9

Fourth Printing, 1977

Printed in the United States of America

To

the increasing numbers who are awaking to the potential for the kingdom of God in Christian camping, and who are willing to train themselves to be useful camp counselors under the guidance of the One of whom it is written, "His name shall be called Wonderful, Counselor."

Contents

CHAPTER		PAGE
	Introduction	9
1.	The Trail to Camp	13
2.	The Counselor and the Camp	29
3.	Here They Come!	43
4.	All Together Now	70
5.	Flora, Fauna, and Dan'l Boone	85
6.	Cloudy in the West	93
7.	May I See You—Alone?	105
8.	The Heart of the Matter	121
9.	Well, They're Gone	136
	Appendix 1: A Word to Camp Directors	149
	Appendix 2: Camp Associations	152
	Sources for Further Information	153

Introduction

The *Camping Guideposts* published in 1962 closed with these words:

> *Camping Guideposts* is not complete, nor will it ever be. A guidepost points toward a destination. Christian camping is an instrument that has proven effective for Christ in our day. Emphasis, facilities, programs and methods will continue to differ widely. It is hoped that camping standards will continue to move upward. As new opportunities are discovered, new guideposts must be erected.
>
> The future will indicate whether *Camping Guideposts* serves a useful purpose. Most books die young, not a few are perpetuated beyond their useful life. Some books merit revision and lengthening of days.

I am delighted for this opportunity to erect a few new guideposts and refurbish the old ones. Camping has changed significantly during the past decade. While much of the first book has been retained, this is essentially a new book. But the purpose identified in the first writing continues; to provide help for the layman who has had the courage to volunteer for camp counseling.

Through the past ten years, I have been deeply involved in Christian camping throughout the United States and Canada. I have visited scores of camps and talked to many hundreds of camp leaders. The conviction I held as I wrote

Camping Guideposts a decade ago has been reinforced again and again—the counselor is the key to effective Christion camping.

A good counselor must first of all be a good person. Now and then I have observed gifted, well-trained leaders completely missing the target, while novice counselors with warm hearts won the campers' loyalty and love. I hope *Camping Guideposts* will warm your heart and provide basic counseling know-how. If that happens, miracles will occur.

Miracles are what *Camping Guideposts* is all about, the miracle of life in Christ Jesus. Where miracles are not happening in campers' lives, the camp is failing in its purpose. No agency of Christendom has greater potential for evangelism and training in godliness than camping. And no camp staff member has greater miracle potential than the counselor. In a real sense, the whole camp revolves around the cabin group with its counselor. If he fails, camp is weakened.

Christian camps come in all sizes and kinds. We applaud the work of those large, well-known camps across the land. But tucked away by small lakes and in farmlands, in mountain valleys and on desert fringes, are the small, unheralded camps that serve many thousands of campers. Their leaders struggle with the same kinds of problems faced by larger camps. Frequently the small camp's resources are severely limited. All the leaders may be volunteers serving for a one-week period, most of them lacking any formal training in camp leadership. I pray they may find help in *Camping Guideposts*.

I have gleaned from the experiences of thirty years in

Introduction

Christian camping what I think are the basics of good camping. I don't expect the experts to agree always, and that is proper. I have not bothered much with scholarly apparatus, because several books exist for the scholar. But not too much can be found for the housewife or merchant who volunteers a week's ministry in camp. I gladly risk the disdain of the scholar to serve the brave volunteer.

One theme flows through the book. *Camp is for the camper.* If a reading of *Camping Guideposts* fixes that in your heart, I will be satisfied. Good counseling is mainly applied common sense anyhow, and when the direction has been correctly established, the destination is generally assured.

I have omitted certain kinds of material usually included in books for counselors, because these matters belong in other books such as directors' manuals and program specialists' books. I have written about methods and ideas I have found useful personally, or have observed others using successfully. Here and there I have tossed in an anecdote that may illustrate the discussion.

Following each chapter, you will find a study guide made up of a series of questions or requests for your opinion. These must not be viewed as tests; rather, they are tools to assist you in thinking through the content of each chapter. Frequently you will be asked for value judgments, or for information you must secure outside the chapter. Often you will be asked to reply with data supplied by the camp you will serve. Where this data is not available, you may wish to respond from your general knowledge, or ignore the question.

Many responses cannot be graded right or wrong. You

may challenge my conclusions. The purpose of the study guide is not that you will agree with me or even display mastery of the chapter. Writing, like talking, is often obscure to the reader or listener. You may be sure the responses of trainees will be eagerly sought as a means of clarifying the text in another revision should Providence and the publisher permit. Your responses will indicate whether you are thinking; and if serious thought concerning the deep implications of camp counseling takes place, *Camping Guideposts* has achieved its primary goal.

You may find occasions when my viewpoint conflicts with the philosophy of your camp. Abide by your camp's philosophy, though I'll not yield until I hear the arguments. You may find it useful to review the study guide prior to reading a chapter. The study guide is, in effect, an overview. Perhaps you will discover that you grasp the ideas of the chapter already. Then you will not feel compelled to dwell too long in its pages.

After completing the chapter, *write* your responses on a separate sheet of paper or in a notebook, with this book open to those pages where you think the answer lies. If you can't find the answer, the question is badly put and the blame is mine, except in those instances where I call for your judgment or data to be supplied by others.

I urge you to seek out other camping books, both secular and Christian-oriented. Several excellent titles have appeared since I first put this book together. You'll find them listed in the bibliography. Master every camping skill you can, but above all, master the skill of guiding campers to Christ. If you find these guideposts helpful in accomplishing this, my purpose is achieved.

1
The Trail to Camp

THIRTY YEARS AGO on a chill dark night in camp, I vowed a solemn vow. Never again would I permit anybody to talk me into counseling at camp. I have renewed that vow two or three times each year since, usually on chill dark nights. Yet I keep returning to camp, even though pain is never far off. Few sorrows known to man have escaped me. Strange sounds in the night. Salt in my coffee. Canoe paddles and even a whole canoe spirited away! And that sudden illness at the far end of the cabin on a dark night, always coincidental with acute flashlight failure. I vow my vow again.

But then in the morning some camper grants me the benediction of a shy smile, and my vow is forgotten. I expect I'll keep on camping for as many years as the Lord grants strength. Life offers few joys to compare with this delightful business of camp counseling.

You won't likely succeed as a counselor unless you accept some misery along with the pleasure. Fair-weather counselors aren't worth much. But camp offers more sun than rain and more joy than pain. If you understand fairly well what Christian camping is all about and learn well the role of a counselor, neither rain nor pain will discourage you.

As a necessary prelude to a more detailed study of camping, let's follow the pathway of introspection. Mastering the machinery of camping is of little worth, if a proper groundwork has not been laid in the heart. *Who* you are and what you are willing to become is infinitely more important than the skills you gain.

Take Uncle John Libke, a retired streetcar conductor from Detroit. For many years he has ministered to kids as counselor and Bible teacher. Uncle John doesn't know much about archery or Ping-Pong, probably less about woodcraft. He just loves kids. When he paces up and down before his four-by-eight-foot flannel board telling Bible adventures, the campers sit up straight and still. Who cares if Uncle John splits an infinitive now and then?

Then the story ends, and Uncle John issues a simple invitation. "You who would like to talk about taking Jesus as Saviour, come along," and Uncle John walks out. Three or four kids follow; sometimes one, or none. But every heart respectfully follows Uncle John. Night and day he moves about the camp, enjoying the company of campers.

Right now, out there somewhere, are ten or twelve kids who are concerned about one big problem. They plan to go to camp, and they wonder who will be their counselor. They are wondering about you! These kids will come from all kinds of homes. They will bring all manner of challenges to your cabin. You, more than anyone else, will determine what camp will be like for these youngsters. Will it be just another funtime with peaks and valleys? Or will camp be a launching pad, thrusting some into a spiritual trajectory higher than you can imagine? It's rather frightening to consider how much depends on you.

The Trail to Camp

One Sunday, Ted Stockfish was reporting to our men's class on his week at junior camp. Ted was aglow. "Man, what a week! In every cabin where we had a solid counselor, boys were saved." Then the glow faded. "But in some cabins, bad news." There were tears in Ted's eyes. He loves kids.

Good counselors always seem in short supply. My prayer is that you will accept this calling from God and become a good counselor.

Let's look at three foundations for effective counseling. Then we'll examine God's purpose for Christian camping and see how that purpose includes you.

FOUNDATIONS FOR EFFECTIVE COUNSELING

Three adults surrounded Millie in a corner of the darkened chapel: the camp director, the camp pastor, and Millie's counselor. The topic was ten dollars which had turned up missing from a suitcase in Millie's cabin just when Millie had suddenly displayed a burst of philanthropy.

Tears streaked twelve-year-old Millie's face. She shivered in her thin, faded dress. No, she hadn't stolen the money! Her aunt sent it to her in the mail. But Millie had not received a letter all week. Well, it wasn't in the *mail*, but in a letter a friend had left when she visited. Millie couldn't remember where her aunt lived, certainly not her phone number, or even exactly when the friend had visited. Finally Millie admitted lying, because she knew no one would believe she had found the money down by the beach. What time? Where?

The camp pastor applied theology, warning Millie of

the consequences of unconfessed sin. The camp director tried psychology, assuring Millie full forgiveness if she confessed; but if she didn't, she must be sent home as a thief. Then Millie's counselor overflowed with compassion. She drew Millie close and whispered, "Millie, we love you."

A little love beats theology and psychology any day. Millie wept her confession. It was a sad little story—a foster child without friends or money, a sister camper ignoring the rule about cash in the cabin, the euphoria of buying treats and friendship. Millie desperately needed love. A counselor supplied that love, because she enjoyed her campers.

The first foundation for good counseling is that you *enjoy campers.* Kathy Nicoll of Inter-Varsity Pioneer Ranch in Calgary, Alberta, Canada, points up a common confusion among camp leaders. She reminds that many adults who talk piously about *loving* kids don't *enjoy* them. There's a difference.

Counseling is not for you if a cabin full of campers unnerves you. You'd better apply for some other kind of camp job. Campers sense a leader's inner hostility that outshouts the best rehearsed speech. If you don't enjoy kids, don't sign up to be a counselor.

Being able to enjoy campers doesn't mean there will never be a chill dark night. All who spend a few years camping with kids have a few hard times. But basically if you enjoy youth and feel comfortable with them, you know that although dark nights come, the sun will shine again.

Enjoying campers does not suggest that you abandon adulthood. Campers don't want a buddy, but a counselor.

The Trail to Camp

What sounds more silly than an adult salting his talk with the latest youth jargon? While remaining thoroughly adult, you can live with youngsters and provide the mood that makes for a happy group.

The second foundation for effective camp counseling is the capacity to *surrender self-interests*. How many push-ups you can perform has little to do with counseling. Neither has marksmanship at archery or mastery of woodlore. Too many counselors exploit campers as a captive audience. *Camp is for campers!*

Surrendering self-interests means that you continually manage yourself for the well-being of your campers. Your only rights are those essential to maintaining health and mental equilibrium. The camp director should provide counselors occasional islands of peace in the turbulent camp sea, but only when his campers are under the care of other staff persons.

This camping foundation creates problems, because the kind of person who volunteers for counseling usually brings broad interests to camp with him. He is gregarious, hence the temptation to socialize with other staff persons at the expense of campers. He is often competitive, hence the urge to play rather than teach campers to play.

Many campers have been afflicted with the fisherman-counselor, an unfortunate blend. Fishermen, ordinarily persons of integrity and high purpose, often suffer the compulsions of an addict. The sternest self-discipline must be imposed to avoid rowing off with two or three campers who must spend a miserable afternoon watching the counselor fish. Teaching campers how to fish is surely a noble form of education, but let the counselor lock his personal tackle in the car! Similarly the table tennis champ. Let him teach, not play.

A certain scoutmaster, it is reported, served faithfully for forty years. He built the best fires and pitched the trimmest tents; he cooked the finest meals and tied the strongest knots. Then he died. And they say the boys haven't been bored since.

Surrendering self-interest is hardest toward the close of camp when the counselors' energies noticeably lag behind the campers'! But few people die from lack of sleep, and much mischief is done during a counselor's clandestine naps, so keep alert! The program must go on.

A general rule holds that counselors should never do anything campers are capable of doing, either work or play. Campers deserve every learning and growth experience the camp can afford. Watching a camper grow in confidence as he masters new skills is one of the counselor's rewards.

A final foundation remains to be considered; the counselor must *accept personal accountability*. Come what may, you are responsible for fulfilling the camp's objectives in your campers. When a camper fails to achieve these objectives, the counselor has failed in some measure.

Sometimes you must compensate for weakness in other leaders, for a bad day in the kitchen, or a solid week of rain. That's a tall order. Developing contingency plans for emergencies strengthens the probability for success.

And sometimes you will fail. Several times I have been forced to send a camper home. I lacked the skill and perception to redirect his attitude into acceptable channels. I lost him. This is the ultimate failure. What more could

The Trail to Camp

I have done? I don't know. In my judgment the camper had to go home to protect those who remained. There seemed to be no alternative. Perhaps another time I will have better insights to help the camper, like Millie's counselor.

Personal accountability suggests goals by which to measure success. One goal is *fun*. Camp must be fun for the camper, else why come? A man challenged me on this in a workshop one day. He pounded the table and growled, "We don't send kids to camp to have *fun!*"

I understood. This man felt camp should seek *spiritual* results: conversions, dedications, and commitments to missionary service. What place had *fun* in the grim business of escaping hell?

But youth's eschatology is somewhat limited. Campers seem more taken with passages that talk about the joy of the Lord. If camp isn't fun, they won't be back. Accountability requires that camp be as much fun as possible.

Of course spiritual gains are not alien to fun. Pleasant days create a spiritually receptive mood. Personal encounters with God for every camper, make up the major camp goal; and such encounters are a part of all lesser goals: good food, adequate facilities, competent leadership, and fun.

Your accountability holds eternal consequences. It is claimed that each year camp produces more significant spiritual decisions than any other church-related activity. Another chapter will discuss some of the reasons for this, but now we simply recognize the fact. Your task is to provide the best possible setting for each of your campers to hear God speak.

Probably you will be asked to write a report on each camper, evaluating his response to camp. This demands careful observation and records to provide information for follow-up. But there is that other record, the accurate one kept by God. Leading campers to Christ is the crowning measure of accountability.

Accountability presumes a willingness to prepare thoroughly. While nothing mysterious or difficult surrounds the role of camp counseling, a great deal of information must be assimilated and some new skills must be mastered, if you are to help your campers gain full value from camp.

Having learned the fundamentals of the task, the best way to refine your knowledge is to practice personal godliness. Most counseling techniques are simply common sense. They include applying love, patience, humility, and having the constant openness of spirit that all effective workers with youth must possess.

This book and others will give you the experiences of others. Beyond what common sense provides and what you can learn from others, you will encounter the quiet working of God. Your final accountability is to Him.

These then are foundations for effective counseling: enjoying your campers, surrendering self-interests, and accepting personal accountability. Since God has called you, you can trust Him to equip you for the work.

Tools for Camp Counseling

Collecting a hundred kids in assorted buildings by a lake does not constitute Christian camping. Organizing cabin groups under responsible counselors still falls short. There are certain relationships and procedures, tested through

The Trail to Camp 21

more than a century of Christian camping, which promise spiritual success. Here are the tools you must work with.

The basic tool is *you*. Beginning counselors sometimes imagine that a collection of skits, stunts, and rainy-day games assures success. Would it were so! There are no surefire gimmicks. There is only *you*. You are unique, a gift from God to the world, with a blending of capabilities possessed by no other. You must be yourself to succeed, just yourself. You will of course work on any unpleasant characteristics such as laziness (which we all share), undue modesty (not nearly as common), or an evil temper. Every Christian must manage himself as God's steward. In camp *you* are the basic tool in the counselor's kit.

The impact of camp is not program or facilities but people. Some fit comfortably into the counselor's role; others belong elsewhere; for long after games and adventure are forgotten, campers will remember their counselor.

A middle-aged minister once counseled a young man through several years of Bible camp. The minister played ball with him, though not particularly well. He scolded him when necessary. He guided him in devotions and gave much time to just chatting. He encouraged the resolve he saw in the young man to pursue the ministry.

One August afternoon the phone rang in a gas station where the young man worked. "Lloyd? How are you? I was just thinking about you. How is it with your soul?"

"Fine, just fine!" I replied. "Everything's fine." And it was. At that moment everything became fine, though through the days and weeks before that phone call, nothing was fine. It is very probable that I am struggling with sentences at my typewriter this moment because this camp counselor cared about me enough to phone. But before he could rescue me through a brief, miraculously-timed phone conversation, he had prepared the way by being a man of God in my presence at camp.

Out of your personal life and preparation will emerge the second counselor's tool, the *cabin atmosphere*. The impact of the small group on the individual is gaining increasing attention. Camp leaders have known about this all along. Helping cabinmates relate warmly to one another creates the spirit that builds a great camp.

Not everything that goes on in camp will be shared as a cabin group. But several times every day, the cabin group comes together, and each evening that cherished— or dreaded—moment comes. It is a mistake to program the camp so strenuously that there are no relaxed moments for the counselor and his cabin group. A proper cabin atmosphere relieves the dread of lights-out.

Many unrelated stimuli attack the camper's mind each day: encounters on the ball field, tensions in craft class when something goes wrong, squabbles with another camper, lessons in Bible class, sermons in chapel. The sorting and absorbing of values await a reflective moment when the camper's heart and mind react. Often you will hear campers say, "I was lying on my bunk thinking about what you said, and . . ."

Later on we will outline details for cabin activity and discover ways to build a wholesome cabin spirit. That spirit is essential to achieving camp goals in your campers. It is a vital tool in your kit.

The most versatile tool is the *camp program*. If more counselors understood this, their work would be less tax-

The Trail to Camp

ing. Your assignment requires that you do all in your power to relate each camper to as much of the camp program as he can absorb. This will fill his hours to overflowing.

This program tool contains the secret of all good camps. If the counselor does not understand it, campers will gain little of value from much that awaits them on the campsite. Young campers especially need encouragement and help to enter into activities. The counselor can set the mood for the shy camper. Recognition of an achievement or of a craft, even though inexpertly done, may be the highlight of the day for one of your campers.

Moving helpfully among your campers throughout the day, establishes friendships that prepare the way for cabin-centered moments. Knowing the content of the chapel message or Bible class provides a natural opening for cabin devotions. The total camp program is a tool to be utilized with great care, for it provides the counselor with daily opportunities to demonstrate the spiritual principles taught in class and chapel.

Cabin devotions is a tool for refining your work as a counselor. It is unfortunate that more care is not taken to coordinate cabin devotions with Bible class and chapel. A strange notion prevails that the more ideas put forth, the more learning takes place. It is truth *grasped*, not truth set forth, that changes lives. Spiritual truth is perceived by the spirit, not the mind. That's why merely repeating a salvation formula does not assure one is saved. Campers will often learn more from the attitudes of leaders than from the lessons they teach. The quiet, informal, cabin devotion may be the moment of spiritual perception.

Another strange notion is the secular-sacred viewpoint, which suggests that camp offers *spiritual* things and other things. Bible class, prayer meetings, chapel, missionary hour, are "spiritual." All else is "other things," with negligible worth. How foolish! For the Christian, Christ pervades all of life all of the time. Every relationship, each tear, every burst of laughter, all mystery, adventure, play, or luxurious loafing must partake of the quality called *spiritual*. God's Spirit does not hide in chapel awaiting the camper's arrival. God is just as interested in the overnight hike as He is in the missionary moment. How many missionaries have heard God's call on the wilderness trail! How many have discovered God's greatness in a thunderstorm. How many have sensed Christ's love through a helping hand up a steep place. Campers should be taught the "everywhereness" of God.

Yet campers need to be taught a disciplined devotional life. While all of life is truly spiritual, not all is *devotional,* and devotions are vital. The cabin group provides an excellent setting for teaching a meaningful devotional life.

We are all familiar with the fagot ceremony. "I promised the Lord last year at camp . . . but I failed." Most often the lack of personal devotions accounts for spiritual failure for both campers and leaders. Until a Christian cultivates a personal life with God, he must subsist on another's gospel. Regular personal Bible reading and prayer renders the Christian self-sustaining before the Lord. Sharpen the tool of devotion.

A final counselor's tool calls us back to the beginning of our discussion. This tool lies beyond the command of man. It is the *sovereign purpose of God*. Ultimately, if God's

The Trail to Camp

work is to be done, God must do it. Little tricks to bolster camp "spiritual" statistics are futile. Decisions growing out of anything other than the Holy Spirit's moving are worthless. Recording camp decisions is fine, but the only authentic statistics are kept in heaven.

Where the Bible is faithfully taught, spiritual gains can be expected. When Christians pray, spiritual results follow. While God's sovereign purpose is not ours to command, He invites us to become willing instruments in His hands to carry out the divine purpose. Somehow, what we *are* determines how God works! An unspeakable mystery.

OBJECTIVES OF CHRISTIAN CAMPING

We've talked about the basic foundations and tools for effective camp counseling, but unless we determine goals it is impossible to measure progress, or even know when we've arrived! Many kinds of camps offer adventure for young people today. The objective of each kind can be discovered by examining the end result. A music camp trains musicians; a sports camp builds athletes. *A Christian camp produces Christians.* It's that simple.

Christian camping is *Christian* only as long as it retains its evangelistic and Bible teaching qualities. It's true that Christians may be active in other kinds of good camping. We have already warned against identifying one kind of activity as "spiritual" in contrast with "other" activities. The ultimate goal determines a camp's right to call itself Christian in our frame of reference. Christian camping seeks to fulfill the Great Commission in the lives of its campers, to present Christ as Saviour and to teach His ways.

Christian camping cannot settle for less than excellence in method, facility, and program. But as we talk about the many ways to work and play with campers, these remain always the means to the grand goal of winning lost campers to Christ and training them in godliness.

Let me tell you why I believe so completely in Christian camping. It began many years ago on an historic campground in south St. Paul, Minnesota. Red Rock Camp Meeting had continued for more than a century when I got there at the age of thirteen. Red Rock boasted no lake or swimming pool. The recreational program was an occasional choose-up-sides ball game and included as equipment an assortment of unmatched, rusty horseshoes, real ones once worn by horses. Our cabin was an old frame house with running water only when it rained. Throughout the day adults and children mingled with the aged and infants.

Meetings were held several times daily in an open tabernacle with a bark-strewn dirt floor. I recall the spirited singing, the shouting-Methodist preaching, the overpowering praying, and that long walk forward to a crude plank altar where I found new life in Christ. At Red Rock I met Rev. Ed Rieff, the camp leader, who changed my life through a providential phone call six years later.

There was a boy kneeling at an altar, and a man caring enough to befriend the boy, a man living so God could nudge him to make a phone call at the moment of need. That's what Christian camping and Chistian camp counseling are all about.

The Trail to Camp

Many settings other than Bible conferences serve equally well for carrying out the objectives of Christian camping. I have ridden and hiked many mountain trails, and canoed hundreds of wilderness miles. I have preached in tabernacle pulpits and shivered in subzero Alaska camps. The setting is not the thing. The purpose and the people, they are everything.

For all who sense God's purpose for our day, camp has two reciprocal objectives: Christ reaching out through the counselor to touch young lives, and Christ working renewal in the counselor.

Well, out there are ten or twelve kids. They're wondering about you. What they become this summer depends very much on what you are willing to become. Who knows what new secrets God's Spirit may whisper to you? That's the adventure trail that leads to camp. Still following? Now we go beyond foundations, tools, and purpose to look at matters of organization and relationships.

STUDY GUIDE

1. Chapter 1 names three foundations for effective counseling; enjoying your campers, surrendering self-interests and accepting personal accountability. Write a brief paragraph for each one, relating the implications of these ideas to yourself as a counselor.
2. Four basic counseling tools are named: yourself, the cabin atmosphere, the camp program, and God's sovereign purpose. Explain how you feel these tools can be employed in your counseling ministry.
3. The chapter gives a five-word statement describing Christian camping's broad purpose. Why do you feel this statement is adequate or inadequate?

4. Of the many kinds of camping (resident, travel, wilderness, conference, decentralized, etc.) which kinds can properly be called "Christian"?
5. What do you understand by the statement near the close of the chapter, "Camp has two reciprocal objectives"?
6. Write the counselors job description and describe the counselor training program outlined by the camp you will serve.

2

The Counselor and the Camp

WHENEVER CAMP LEADERS GATHER, an argument arises over what constitutes *real camping*. Reaching acceptable definitions usually proves difficult in view of the dynamic qualities of camping. For our purpose we can settle for this: Christian camping is group living in an outdoor setting over an extended time, having spiritual objectives. *Real* camping is any kind that achieves true spiritual objectives.

THE HISTORY OF CAMPING

As far as I can discover, a definitive history of Christian camping has never been published. Several books outline the backgrounds of camping in general, notably A. Viola Mitchell and Ida B. Crawford's *Camp Counseling* (Philadelphia: W. B. Saunders, 1961). Every serious student of camping should read this book. Mitchell and Crawford credit Fredrick William Gunn with organizing the first camp in 1861. Mr. Gunn exploited his pupils' enthusiasm for outdoor living in a variety of educational camping activities through 1879.

In 1876 Dr. Joseph Trimble Rothrock, a physician, experimented with a private health camp, but the experiment failed for lack of revenue. According to Mitchell and Crawford, the first recorded church camp was launched by the Reverend George W. Hinkley in 1880, when he took seven boys on a camping trip to Gardner's Island near Wakefield, Rhode Island. The Reverend Hinkley later founded the Good Will Farm for Boys and offered a program not unlike that found in many Bible camps today.

The camp with the longest continuous history was founded in 1885 by Summer F. Dudley, who later became a YMCA staff member. He continued camping with boys until his death at forty-three in 1897. The camp he was then associated with at Lake Champlain, Westport, New York, was named in his honor.

Yet in my opinion none of these camping pioneers deserves the title, "Grandfather of Christian Camping." That honor goes to some unknown Presbyterian clergyman who proposed to his brethren that a devotional exercise be conducted in northern Kentucky.

CANE RIDGE CAMP MEETING

Somewhere between 1800 and 1801, in the upper part of Kentucky at a memorable place called "Cane Ridge," there was appointed a sacramental meeting by some of the Presbyterian ministers. At the meeting, seemingly unexpected by ministers or people, the mighty power of God was displayed in an extraordinary manner; many were moved to tears and bitter and loud crying for mercy. The meeting was protracted for weeks. Ministers of almost all denominations flocked in from far and near. The meeting was kept up by night and day. Thousands heard of the mighty work, and came on foot, on horseback, in carriages and wagons. It was supposed that there were in attendance at times during the meeting from twelve to twenty-five thousand people. Hundreds fell prostrate

The Counselor and the Camp

under the mighty power of God, as men slain in battle. Stands were erected in the woods from which preachers of different churches proclaimed repentance toward God and faith in our Lord Jesus Christ, and it was supposed, by eye and ear witnesses, that between one and two thousand souls were happily and powerfully converted to God during the meeting. It was not unusual for one, two, three, and four to seven preachers be addressing the listening thousands at the same time from the different stands erected for the purpose. The heavenly fire spread in almost every direction. It was said, by truthful witnesses, that at times more than one thousand persons broke out into loud shouting all at once, and that the shouts could be heard for miles around.

From this camp-meeting, for so it ought to be called, the news spread through all the Churches, and through all the land, and it excited great wonder and surprise; but it kindled a religious flame that spread all over Kentucky and through many other states. And I may here be permitted to say, that this was the first camp-meeting ever held in the United States, and here our camp-meetings took their rise.[*]

Now that was a camp! No history of Christian camping dares overlook the impact of the frontier camp meeting on the history of America or the development of the camping movement. Eagle-eyed mothers tried, not always successfully, to keep ardent young swains a respectful distance from the maidens. Grandmothers sought to impress on junior boys the virtues of all-day preaching, also with limited success. Apparently no one had yet considered the potential of camp counselors.

[*] *The Autobiography of Peter Cartwright* (New York: Abingdon), 1956, pp. 33-34. Used by permission.

But with the settling of the frontier and the sophistication of society, camp meetings passed from the raw, emotional spontaneity of Cane Ridge to orderly preaching and prayer conferences. Some survived to become the forerunners of today's Bible conference.

Somewhere along the line, the needs of young people were recognized, and a youth program was introduced. In time, youth camps developed to be refined into today's vigorous Christian camping movement with its wide variety of programs. The idea of Christians gathering outdoors for extended periods with spiritual objectives reaches back to the beginning of the nineteenth century, anticipating other forms of camping by more than sixty years. The influence of camping on the Christian church can scarcely be overemphasized, and I believe camping's greatest days are yet to come.

Organizing for Effective Camps

The problem of definition is equalled by the difficulty of agreeing on the proper system for organizing the camp. The best system is whatever works within a given tradition. The vital concern is that the counselor accept the team concept, however the team is put together.

The simple organizational pattern reported here can be adapted to fit the needs of large or small camps. Job titles and job descriptions will vary. Your task is to learn the duties assigned to a counselor in your camp and to carry out those duties with zeal.

It is probably worthwhile to consider organizational charts, for inevitably you will encounter them. Charts are

The Counselor and the Camp

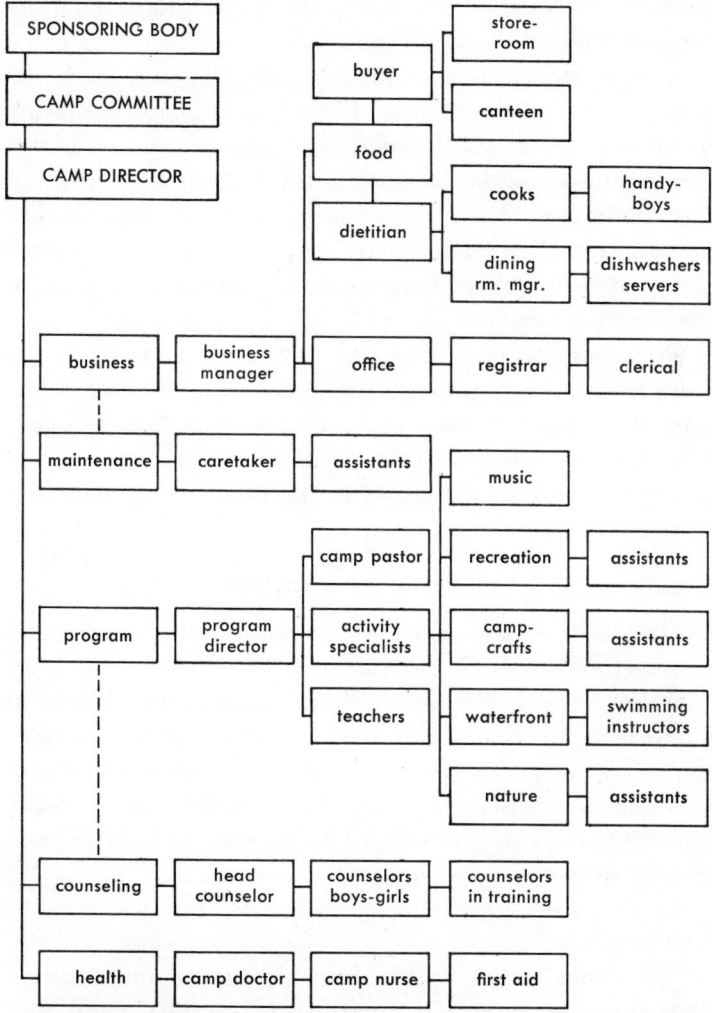

Floyd and Pauline Todd, *Camping for Christian Youth* (New York: Harper, 1963), p. 71. Used by permission.

useful tools, dearly beloved by camp directors, but they are not without some dangers.

A typical chart places the sponsoring agency supreme, just above the camp board. Beneath the board, radiating in all directions, solid and dotted lines dash to and fro connecting directors, committees, assistant directors, and ultimately you. The chart visualizes lines of responsibility and authority, and if you look closely, you find the camper lying wistfully somewhere near the bottom of the page, connected to you.

Here lies the danger of the charts. Organization can loom so large in the minds of leaders that *purpose* is forgotten. *Camp is for the camper.* The objective for every leader is the spiritual good of each camper. It might be helpful to reverse the order in the charts, and place the camper on top.

Camp Staff Positions

Most camps issue a handbook describing the title and responsibility of staff members. Your concern is to learn *function* and *relationships*. The camp dean may be called camp director across the lake. The camp pastor's duties may vary from camp to camp. Discover how each worker functions in your camp, so you can relate effectively to the entire team. The following job descriptions will suggest typical duties.

CAMP DIRECTOR

The camp director is responsible to the organization operating the camp. He coordinates the year-round program, hires salaried personnel, and directs their activities.

The Counselor and the Camp

He looks after business management and grounds maintenance. His is the ultimate responsibility for the total camp program.

PROGRAM DIRECTOR

The program director is responsible to the camp director, and acts as coordinator of the activities of a given week. He looks after all the details not assigned to the camp director. He plans the week's program according to the age of the campers. He may share in recruiting and training staff members, particularly counselors. Staff members are responsible to the program director.

CAMP PASTOR

Sometimes called the camp evangelist or missionary, the camp pastor is the speaker at chapel sessions and is responsible to arrange camp-wide devotional activity. He plans the chapel programs. He considers the spiritual needs of the staff as well as the campers and stands ready to assist counselors in meeting campers' needs. Since he is not associated with administration or discipline, he has a valuable opportunity to serve as a "neutral" advisor in serious camper problems.

CHIEF COUNSELOR

The chief or head counselor may act as assistant to the program director with responsibility for the cabin counselors. Discipline problems are channeled through the chief counselor. In co-ed camps, two chief counselors are appointed, one for the boys, one for the girls. The chief counselor leads daily staff meetings to discover needs and to strengthen the camp program.

ATHLETIC DIRECTOR

The entire recreational program of the camp is under the athletic director's supervision. His staff will include specialists in waterfront activity, field sports, games, and outings. He may be responsible for the camp's nature program. He will seek to insure the supervision and safe conduct of all athletic activity. He may call on counselors and teachers to make his work effective. He will be careful, especially in junior camps, to include a large measure of instruction in the athletic program, teaching youngsters how properly to play, swim, shoot, or row.

CRAFT DIRECTOR

The craft director's job is to plan the craft program, order materials, and teach handcrafts. Crafts play an important role in camping. The endless variety of handcrafts are sometimes viewed with alarm by those who wish to keep the program nature-centered. Nature crafts are finding wider use as experienced leaders are developed. Craft work fills empty hours, especially for campers less interested in active sports.

FOOD SERVICE DIRECTOR

Usually the chief cook or the dietitian is the director of food service. The preparation and serving of food is the responsibility of this person. Assistant cooks and kitchen helpers share in this important part of camp life. Campers are used in some camps for dining room cleanup, setting tables, and washing dishes. Many states require persons handling food to possess special health certificates.

CAMP CARETAKER

The camp caretaker has the duty of caring for the camp buildings and grounds. Matters needing his attention should be reported immediately to the program director. Leaking faucets, broken windows, sagging doors, or hazardous conditions are everyone's concern, but the proper person should make all repairs.

CAMP NURSE

The camp nurse is the one qualified to care for the ill. All injuries, no matter how slight, should be referred to her. *Take* campers to the nurse, don't send them. Campers and counselors should turn in to the nurse all medications—even aspirin—avoiding accidental mixing of pills, or dangerous pranks. Health problems should be recorded with the nurse on arrival at camp. She will have supplies for bed-wetters. The slightest hint of illness should be reported. Most states require camp nurses to have at least the certificate of LPN or LVN.

TEACHERS

The teachers' basic job is to lead Bible studies. Bible study forms an important part of Christian camping. In many camps, the counselors conduct Bible studies with their cabin groups, a most effective approach. In other camps, teaching specialists may be assigned to Bible classes made up of several cabin groups. Teachers, like counselors, may be asked to share on a limited basis in other program areas.

COUNSELOR

The counselor is responsible to the chief counselor for the campers assigned to his cabin, usually numbering eight to twelve. The counselor looks after the health, safety, and spiritual welfare of his cabin group and helps the camper gain maximum benefit from the program. The counselor leads in cabin devotions and remains alert to opportunities for personal guidance. The counselor sees spiritual values in every part of camp life. He will prepare an evaluation report for each camper in his group. The counselor works as part of a team, each member contributing toward winning the camper to Christ and leading him to spiritual maturity.

THE COUNSELOR AND THE CAMP STAFF

A careful, continuing study of Romans 12 will equip you well for serving on the camp team. Read this chapter several times a day through the weeks preceding camp. *Living Letters* offers a particularly refreshing interpretation of Romans 12:6a: "God has given each of us the ability to do certain things well." This is a good word for you as a counselor, suggesting that God has given you special gifts and that others also have particular gifts. Don't make the mistake of attempting to do everyone's work!

Interfering with other counselors or staff members creates tension. Unless the safety of a camper is at stake, avoid involvement in other cabin groups. You may indeed

The Counselor and the Camp

beam a stern eye at a chapel offender, or gently redirect energies that threaten the peace of the canteen line, but respect the leadership responsibilities of each staff member.

You might pause extra long at Romans 12:18. *Living Letters* again paraphrases the meaning aptly. "Don't quarrel with anyone. Be at peace with everyone, just as much as you possibly can." Ill feelings between leaders are quickly felt by campers, so why not extend your ministry to fellow workers as well as campers? Since leaders are quite human, they experience low moments. Absorbing a staff member's temporary irritation can enrich you and that staff member. A quarrel has never arisen that would not end immediately if one party simply ceased talking.

Respect the chain of command. Sometimes you will be tempted to flee to the camp director with a grievance that should be taken to your head counselor. Or you may feel like scolding the maintenance man. Resist the urge to complain about the state of the oatmeal. The cook already knows the oatmeal is scorched, and the anguish in the kitchen exceeds yours.

Unpleasant assignments may fall to you. Do them quickly and without complaint, even though others seem to escape such duty. Romans 12 speaks of a "living sacrifice." That which is sacrificed is beyond complaining. Some camps cannot afford a janitor. The sight of a counselor polishing a toilet bowl with a brush, a smile, and a song will speak to the heart of a camper, and that might be the mystic moment of discovery. Who can tell?

The Counselor and the Counselor-in-Training

You may be asked to work with a counselor-in-training (CIT), or a junior counselor. The development of new leaders is one of Christian camping's major contributions to the church. Many camps pursue an aggressive program to grow their own leaders. While this places an extra burden on you, the task should be accepted cheerfully.

A full discussion of the CIT properly belongs in a camp administration manual. Be prepared to give willing leadership when a CIT is assigned to you. Many successful CIT programs place trainees in housing apart from campers, with visits to cabins for specific training purposes. Some camps place trainees in the cabin as an assistant counselor. But beware of making the trainee half camper and half leader, a situation with potential problems.

One problem arises when a counselor assigns the more unpleasant tasks to the trainee, or overloads him with duties. The proper approach finds the counselor and trainee working side-by-side, sharing leadership under the counselor's guidance.

A second problem can result when a trainee joins forces with the campers and polarizes the cabin group, sometimes negating the counselor's efforts. If this situation is discovered, the counselor should take immediate corrective steps through proper channels. A CIT progam must never be allowed to interfere with the spiritual well-being of campers, the primary purpose of camp.

A well-structured, properly supervised CIT program belongs in camping as a natural extension of the camp's spiritual ministry. The cabin counselor becomes part of the teaching team, leading veteran campers into the joys of leadership.

The Counselor and Personal Growth

Provision will be made for the counselor's relaxation and personal growth. The one-week counselor might not feel the need of renewal, but those who serve for several weeks find it imperative! Time off should be scrupulously observed, preferably away from the center of camp activity.

Staff meetings for discussion, training, and prayer are invaluable means for personal growth. Sharing concerns and victories distributes the burdens and blessings of your cabin through the entire staff. Aggressive participation in staff meetings is one of the counselor's assignments. While Proverbs 11:14 probably refers to circumstances other than camp, it seems appropriate to borrow the idea here. "In the multitude of counselors there is safety." Many a rebel camper has been tamed through a staff prayer meeting.

All Christian leaders suffer the danger of self-neglect in the busyness of serving others. Cultivate a constant attitude of prayer. Discipline your time to include daily personal devotions, perhaps in company with your campers. The counselor who maintains a quiet, constant dialogue with his own spirit concerning matters of faith and godliness, finds a source of strength unknown by those who allow themselves to become completely mastered by leadership burdens.

The Counselor and His Campers

A proper relationship to the camp staff and program is vital, yet you are called again to remember the primary concern of the counselor: that handful of campers who share your cabin. If I seem to overemphasize this, be assured it is deliberate. The issues are too grave to treat casually. Campers may be calloused or scatterbrained or blustering, or weepy—and you will find all these and more—but they are what camp is all about. We'll plunge into this matter in the next chapter.

STUDY GUIDE

1. In a few sentences, describe the pioneer camp meeting and explain why it deserves the title, "Grandfather of Christian Camping."
2. Construct a simple organizational chart for the camp you will serve, or for a typical Christian camp. Trace the line of responsibility from sponsoring agency to camper.
3. Briefly describe the responsibilities of the key leaders in the camp you will serve, or the staff positions listed in chapter 2.
4. Explain the advantages found in requiring a counselor also to be Bible teacher in his cabin group.
5. List several provisions and admonitions from Romans 12 that are appropriate for camp counselors.
6. What is the counselor's role in the counselor-in-training program? What are the possible problems?
7. What steps should the counselor take to guard against neglecting his spiritual growth while at camp?

3

Here They Come!

ONE OF THE MORE UNNERVING MOMENTS in my brief career as a substitute teacher, occurred in an elementary school in Michigan. The principal handed me the day's assignment with unusual solicitude. I was to teach *kindergarten*! That proved to be the longest day in my life as a teacher, one I never allowed to happen again.

My problem was neither a lack of concern nor sincerity. I just didn't understand little kids. You can expect trials of like magnitude if you fail to acquaint yourself with the characteristics of your campers. Every group will contain one or more youngsters laden with exceptions. Sometimes you may think *none* of your campers is normal, but ordinarily you will succeed in meeting day-by-day challenges if you learn to know your campers.

The developmental characteristics listed on pages 44-49 are reprinted from *These Are Your Children* by Jenkins, Schacter, and Bauer.* You should secure this book and study it carefully (see Sources for Further Information). The authors give the following advice:

> Children are not small adults. They do not think, feel, or react as adults do. They do not have the knowledge, judgment, or background to choose experiences that will

*Reprinted by permission of the publisher.

be beneficial to them and to reject those that may be harmful. At the same time we cannot judge or measure them by adult standards. Children need grown-ups who can thoughtfully lead the way through the confusion of our times. The first responsibility of those who sincerely want to help children to grow up ready to take their part in this changing world is to try to understand the world of children; the general pattern according to which all children grow and, within this framework, the individual needs and characteristics of each particular child for whom they are responsible.†

ABOUT EIGHT

Physical Development

Growth still slow and steady—arms lengthening, hands growing.
Eyes ready for both near and far vision.
　Near-sightedness may develop this year.
Permanent teeth continuing to appear.
Large muscles still developing. Small muscles better developed, too. Manipulative skills are increasing.
Attention span getting longer.
Poor posture may develop.

Characteristic Behavior

Often careless, noisy, argumentative, but also alert, friendly, interested in people.
More dependent on his mother, less so on his teacher. Sensitive to criticism.
New awareness of individual differences.
Eager, more enthusiastic than cautious. Higher accident rate.

†Jenkins, Schacter, and Bauer, *These Are Your Children*, p. 11. Used by permission.

Gangs beginning. Best friends of same sex.
Allegiance to other children instead of to an adult in case of conflict.
Greater capacity for self-evaluation.
Much spontaneous dramatization, ready for simple classroom dramatics.
Understanding of time and use of money.
Responsive to group activities, both spontaneous and adult-supervised.
Fond of team games, comics, television, movies, adventure stories, collections.

SPECIAL NEEDS

Praise and encouragement from adults.
Reminders of his responsibilities.
Wise guidance and channeling of his interests and enthusiasms, rather than domination or unreasonable standards.
A best friend.
Experience of belonging to peer group—opportunity to identify with others of same age and sex.
Adult-supervised groups and planned after-school activities.
Exercise of both large and small muscles.

ABOUT NINE OR TEN

PHYSICAL DEVELOPMENT

Slow, steady growth continues—girls forge further ahead. Some children reach the plateau preceding the preadolescent growth spurt.
Lungs as well as digestive and circulatory systems almost mature. Heart especially subject to strain.

Teeth may need straightening. First and second bicuspids appearing.

Eye-hand coordination good. Ready for crafts and shop work.

Eyes almost adult size. Ready for close work with less strain.

CHARACTERISTIC BEHAVIOR

Decisive, responsible, dependable, reasonable, strong sense of right and wrong.

Individual differences distinct, abilities now apparent.

Capable of prolonged interest. Often makes plans and goes ahead on his own.

Gangs strong, of short duration and changing membership. Limited to one sex.

Perfectionist—wants to do well, but loses interest if discouraged or pressured.

Interested less in fairy tales and fantasy, more in his community and country and in other countries and peoples.

Loyal to his country and proud of it.

Spends a great deal of time in talk and discussion. Often outspoken and critical of adults, although still dependent on adult approval.

Frequently argues over fairness in games.

Wide discrepancies in reading ability.

SPECIAL NEEDS

Active rough and tumble play.

Friends and membership in a group.

Training in skills, but without pressure.

Books of many kinds, depending on individual reading level and interest.

Reasonable explanations without talking down.
Definite responsibility.
Frank answers to his questions about coming physiological changes.

THE PREADOLESCENT

Physical Development

A "resting period," followed by a period of rapid growth in height and then growth in weight. This usually starts sometime between 9 and 13. Boys may mature as much as two years later than girls.
Girls usually taller and heavier than boys.
Reproductive organs maturing. Secondary sex characteristics developing.
Rapid muscular growth.
Uneven growth of different parts of the body.
Enormous but often capricious appetite.

Characteristic Behavior

Wide range of individual differences in maturity level.
Gangs continue, though loyalty to the gang stronger in boys than in girls.
Interest in team games, pets, television, radio, movies, comics. Marked interest differences between boys and girls.
Teasing and seeming antagonism between boys' and girls' groups.
Awkwardness, restlessness, and laziness common as result of rapid and uneven growth.
Opinion of own group beginning to be valued more highly than that of adults.
Often becomes overcritical, changeable, rebellious, uncooperative.

Self-conscious about physical changes.
Interested in earning money.

Special Needs

Understanding of the physical and emotional changes about to come.

Skillfully planned school and recreation programs to meet needs of those who are approaching puberty as well as those who are not.

Opportunities for greater independence and for carrying more responsibility without pressure.

Warm affection and sense of humor in adults. No nagging, condemnation, or talking down.

Sense of belonging, acceptance by peer group.

THE ADOLESCENT

Physical Development

Rapid weight gain at beginning of adolescence. Enormous appetite.

Sexual maturity, with accompanying physical and emotional changes. Girls are usually about two years ahead of boys.

Sometimes a period of glandular imbalance.

Skeletal growth completed, adult height reached, muscular coordination improved.

Heart growing rapidly at beginning of period.

Characteristic Behavior

Going to extremes, emotional instability with "know-it-all" attitude.

Return of habits of younger child—nail biting, tricks, impudence, day-dreaming.

Here They Come!

High interest in philosophical, ethical, and religious problems. Search for ideals.

Preoccupation with acceptance by the social group. Fear of ridicule and of being unpopular. Oversensitiveness and self-pity.

Strong identification with an admired adult.

Assertion of independence from family as a step toward adulthood.

Responds well to group responsibility and group participation. Groups may form cliques.

High interest in physical attractiveness.

Girls usually more interested in boys than boys in girls, resulting from earlier maturing of the girls.

SPECIAL NEEDS

Acceptance by and conformity with others of own age.

Adequate understanding of sexual relationships and attitudes.

Kind, unobtrusive, adult guidance which does not threaten the adolescent's feeling of freedom.

Assurance of security. Adolescents seek both dependence and independence.

Opportunities to make decisions and to earn and save money.

Provision for constructive recreation. Some cause, idea, or issue to work for.

These charts summarize general characteristics which will suggest behavioral responses typical of the age-groupings commonly found in camp. You should understand that this is only a general guide. Many campers will exhibit some degree of variance. Unfortunately, you cannot rely on campers to mature at the same rate. There must be a careful appraisal of each individual. But if you know how a *typical* junior, junior high, or high school camper can be expected to respond, you can lead with confidence.

Obviously your approach to leadership must be adjusted to the capabilities of your group. A first-year camper must be treated gently. This may be his first extended stay away from home and mother. A high school senior requires near adult treatment. He will be offended by any form of juvenile treatment.

Several sources for additional information on age-level characteristics are listed in the Sources for Further Information. I cannot stress too much the importance of this matter. Expecting too much or too little from campers is a primary source of counselor failures.

A knowledge of the general characteristics should be followed by a continuing effort to discover the nature and needs of each camper. The lower the camper-counselor ratio, the greater the potential for effective work. Begin by learning each camper's name. A name tag will prove helpful for the first day. You may wish to offer some honor to the camper who first identifies every cabinmate by name. Use the camper's name each time you speak to him. Post a cabin roster identifying campers by bed location.

Bear in mind that campers are discovering your characteristics at the same time you are learning theirs. The age-old struggle between youth and authority sets in, as well as the inevitable tussle for sovereignty within the peer group. Your campers will probably know you before you know them. The first hour will go far toward establishing your leadership.

Here They Come!

Campers will type you as friendly, approachable, fun-loving; or stiff, authoritarian, or aloof. First impressions are slow to change. If you sincerely love your campers and enjoy being with them, they will respond with friendship. But don't think love demands overfamiliarity. Be slow to allow campers first-name privileges unless you are quite near their age, though local traditions may alter this.

Most campers will be anxious to please you, though a few will go to great lengths to hide the fact. A few campers may resist you, and you cannot force your way into their friendship. A camper's first response to your leadership often reveals basic spiritual needs. Sloppy Sue's bunk is a mess. Apple-polishing Anne dogs your steps. Shy Sharon needs your attention though she hides from you. Grumpy Gertie pouts on her lower bunk, coveting the more favorable altitude of Sneaky Sal's upper bunk. Sneaky Sal has secreted a contraband radio in the niche where roof meets wall. The characteristics of individual campers begin to emerge as the cabin group takes shape. This is your challenge for the week.

You must resist the human trait to classify campers in "I-like" and "I-don't-like" groups. And you will not engage in petty contests of will with immature children, contests you can never win. Unlovely campers present your greatest challenge.

You will learn to judge which camper requires more personal attention, and what kind of attention. The withdrawn, shy camper may possess greater possibilities than the extrovert who will take you over if you let him. Use wisdom in pairing off campers as bunkmates. Some camps attempt to separate close friends and campers from a common church home, but I question the wisdom of this. Imposing adult values on youngsters does not always accomplish its purpose; and for some, the only security they find in camp is an established friend.

As soon as possible you will begin to learn background facts about your campers. Some camps provide a camper profile for counselors. Casual conversation and careful listening will reveal much about an individual.

I recall a junior boy named Fred who pegged himself as the bad-news camper by turning the first meal into chaos. Fred's manners were unspeakable. He continually annoyed those seated near him, and he brought down the wrath of his counselors. No one told the counselor that this lad had no father, and his mother entertained a variety of men in the home. Trouble was the normal pattern for this troubled boy, so why change at camp? The first meal established a pattern of hostility that prevailed through the week. It is doubtful the camp did much for Fred. Perhaps his needs were deeper than camp could meet.

Organizing the Cabin Group

Each camp builds cabin traditions that should be honored, plus camp-wide traditions that determine the kind of system you will develop for life in your cabin. Standards for dress, conduct, and conversation may be quite different from those practiced in a camper's home. Since a measure of regimentation is inevitable, the boundaries should be clearly explained.

In spite of much grumbling about rules, campers appreciate guidelines. You may doctor up rules by calling them traditions, which is fine; but whatever the name, make sure campers understand. Encourage questions and discussion. Someone will probably ask about the penalty for breaking rules. The pattern for discipline and your determination to enforce rules should be understood.

There will always be gray areas. Magazines and books of negligible value should be discouraged. Radios and tape recorders should be regulated to preserve a wholesome tone in the camp. Different attitudes prevail concerning smoking. Recognizing the spiritual need of older young people caught up in the smoking habit, some camps designate times and places to smoke. To me it is quite unthinkable that a counselor would indulge this obviously harmful habit. Be alert for the presence of drugs in camp. The prevalence of marijuana and other narcotics among young people makes it inevitable that some camps must deal with the problem.

Equally deadly and as common as drugs, is the infiltration of pornography. Neither problem calls for a response of rage or shock. Addicts of drugs and pornography desperately need Christ. You can expect both problems to crop up in camp, especially among older groups. A pattern should be determined to deal with both problems.

Older campers may drive private cars to camp. Ordinarily car keys are turned in at the time of registration. Staff members should observe automobile regulations also. Rules apply equally to motorcycles.

Occasionally you will find a camper who needs counsel concerning dress standards, on and off the beach. Almost always a kind, firm word will remove the problem. In co-ed camps restricted areas should be clearly defined and wholesome boy-girl interests expected. Dating practices vary in camps, as well as acceptable patterns for social relationships. Overt displays of affection should be discouraged. Counselors sometimes need reminders too! Where campers need help, understanding counsel should be given.

An objective, straightforward discussion of standards for maintaining a wholesome, spiritually enriching atmosphere usually serves better than a detailed list of rules. Where specific boundaries are needed, they should be clearly presented. Let campers know what is expected of them. But what can you do with borderline issues? Some matters do not gracefully lend themselves to legislation. What are *short* shorts? Or when is a modest two-piece bathing suit to be preferred over immodest one-piece attire? Which books and magazines are suitable; what music is acceptable?

The existence of such issues, especially among older campers, provides grist for the counselor's mill. Authoritarian legislation won't prove acceptable in the long run, for this approach has already been exploited in legitimate areas. A candid exploring of issues opens the hearts of both counselor and campers for mutual understanding. Don't expect easy answers; but look for stimulating, creative discussion to help campers discover truth.

I mentioned earlier the failures I have experienced in losing some campers. The maximum camp penalty is expulsion. Campers should know this possibility exists. The counselor's responsibility for discipline should be kept at a minimum, never including corporal punishment. Striking a camper or otherwise inflicting pain may gratify the counselor's momentary wrath, but it seldom achieves any good for the camper. Discipline will be discussed in greater detail later in the chapter.

From Dawn to Dark

Posting an activity schedule in no way assures a happy week for your campers. The schedule is but a skeleton on which you must hang muscle and meat. Younger campers especially need to become involved in camp activities. To a large measure, you become the camp program. A primary role of the counselor is to relate the camper to the total camp program. Campers often overlook activities you ignore.

Most camps expect counselors to spend a major portion of the day with their cabin groups. Perhaps you will be asked to plan the day's program. If so, include your campers in the planning. Aim at variety with the campers' needs and interests in mind, even though your personal aptitudes might lie in other directions.

Aim at maximum involvement for every camper, and work hard in behalf of the reticent group member. Though there may be program specialists in charge, your presence will encourage campers. Friendships built during crafts and play create the climate you need to touch the camper's heart during devotions. And often, in the mysterious manner of God's working, a camper's moment of discovery will come at a nondevotional time. Don't restrict God's Spirit to your worship schedule!

Bear in mind that your camp ministry does not require mastery of every sport or craft. You may be a learner along with your campers, and sometimes you must bow to their superior skill! Nothing pleases a camper more than helping his counselor tie a proper knot or correct an irregular braid.

However you organize your day, spend as much time as possible with your campers, thrusting them as deeply as possible into the total camp program. You may be asked to attend a staff meeting while your campers are under the care of another leader. Or you may be granted a blessed hour for relaxation. Take it! But covet every opportunity to be with your cabin group.

Many camps have adopted the good practice of assigning to counselors the major Bible teaching role. This demands added preparation, but the spiritual potential makes it worthwhile. Other camps retain a more traditional approach, securing Bible teaching specialists just as sports and craft specialists are engaged. Whatever pattern your camp follows, you will find your presence in class and chapel most helpful.

The attention span of campers is discouragingly brief, and the setting for class and worship often includes built-in distractions. Once, high in the Montana Rockies, I witnessed the total frustration of a camp pastor who had launched into an ill-advised prebreakfast sermonette. A log semicircle was inhabited by a hundred hungry, wiggling juniors while the minister unlimbered his abbreviated three-pointer. His sincerity was impeccable, but his communication level barely moved the needle. Then two red squirrels launched a game of tag in the pines immediately over his head. The few who hadn't noticed the squirrels did so when the pastor commanded the campers to stop watching those animals and *pay attention*. I'm not convinced it was the devil who sent those squirrels, as was

Here They Come!

intimated. The event precipitated worthwhile conversation during rest-hour devotions that afternoon, and later on in an informal staff meeting.

The presence of counselors helps campers to gain maximum value from chapel and Bible class. The counselor also gains valuable points of contact for meaningful cabin devotions later in the day. Many camps fail to minister as effectively as they might, simply because of the quantity of unrelated data poured out before the camper each day. Only the truth *perceived* by the camper accomplishes much of lasting value. When you build your cabin devotions upon the ideas presented in class or chapel, you strengthen the probability for spiritual perception. Adding more unrelated ideas, good though they are, may only confuse your campers.

Do not hesitate to sit with campers who seem bent on amusing or annoying one another in chapel. Usually this restores order. Older campers require a bit more subtle treatment. A row of counselors seated apart from a hundred restless campers has little value.

If you would make camp a memorable experience for your cabin group, plan to involve them in as much of the program as possible. Enter into activities with them, paying special heed to the reluctant camper. Share as many of their daily experiences as possible; be among them in Bible study and worship. Watch for spiritual responses, and keep alert for thoughts you can use in cabin devotions.

Enriching Cabin Life

Camp becomes a total experience for most campers, each part enriching the day: the ball field, the beach, the dining hall, the chapel. Every staff member adds his personal contribution to the store of treasures a camper will carry home. The adventure of cabin life rates high in its memory-building potential.

One-by-one your campers gather inside, and the door is finally closed for the night. Then your skill as a counselor is tested, and few tests can compare with the first night!

Even veteran counselors approach the first night in camp with trepidation. Counselors are made of less stern stuff than campers, and welcome the tolling of the lights-out bell. But campers feel otherwise. When you think about it, a bell has little to do with sleep. Campers sleep only when they are sleepy.

Consider the nonsleep factors found that first night at camp. Nothing is like home, where campers live 51 weeks of the year. The group may be composed of people who barely know each other. The struggle to find a place in the peer-group hierarchy has set in. The beds are strange and perhaps uncomfortable. A day of travel and exciting experiences lies behind each camper. And there is the counselor whom tradition dictates campers must test. How futile to intone, "Lights out. Everyone go to sleep."

Turning lights out is comparatively easy (except for flashlights). Inducing sleep is exceedingly difficult. Every camper turns into a ventriloquist with an amazing repertoire of weird sounds. A spirit hurls a tennis shoe through the darkness. An errant frog may have found his way into the counselor's bed. You are no match for a cabin full of juniors, much less a cabin full of high schoolers. You can't lick them, so join them! Make the first night fun.

I have on occasion met an authoritarian person who de-

Here They Come!

clares that *he* tolerates no nonsense from campers the first night in camp. When he says quiet, he means *quiet*. Then I observe him at an adult retreat. He asserts his adult prerogative to ignore the printed schedule which establishes the hour for lights-out and quiet. Extended political or theological debates flow on, on the premise that adults sleep when they grow sleepy. Youthful campers will do likewise.

The secret to success the first night in camp is to help your campers become sleepy. Sensible bedtime hours are vital for health, and equally vital is sensible planning to bring weariness to an optimum level at approximately the same time as the lights-out bell. This requires nothing short of genius.

Agree to limit noise levels to the confines of the cabin. Campers will ordinarily understand the need for this, particularly when they feel that too much noise will bring down the wrath of the head counselor on their cabin counselor. You might suggest that possibility. You might also suggest, for safety sake, that all campers remain in bed after the lights are out. Except for very young campers, explain that any who feel compelled to make an unscheduled excursion to the washroom must go alone.

Extended devotions have a marvelous capacity to induce drowsiness. You may abbreviate them later, but on the first night take full advantage of this resource. You will *not* say, "All you good Christians will go right to sleep." Some of our finest church leaders were holy terrors in camp, particularly the first night. Never threaten what you can't perform. Declaring, "The very next camper who makes a noise will be sent straight home," is an irresistible challenge.

The finest device I know to maintain cabin serenity is a story, a long one. Perhaps your very best story. It may or may not possess a religious lesson. It must not be designed to terrify campers, or even mildly scare them. Perhaps the ghost story has a place in camp, but the first night is surely not that place. If you can introduce a continued story to run all week, happy are you.

There is no surefire formula for gracefully putting campers to sleep the first night. Make them as tired as possible prior to bedtime. Involve them in happy group sharing at bedtime. Then focus their energies through a story until sleep comes. Then you can sleep too.

"Daylight in the Swamp"

This historic cry from the lumber camp has been replaced by the camp bell which rings distressingly early. However, a factor often overlooked by beginning counselors is the early riser, a camper who may anticipate the rising bell by hours. He tends to forget that most of the camp is still sleeping. Explain that all campers are to remain in bed until the rising signal.

Campers rarely need encouragement to get up the first morning, but on succeeding days you must help some. Early rising is a chief contributor to a quiet cabin at lights out, but beware of the camper who naps all afternoon!

Your camp tradition will determine the morning sequence of activities. Flag-raising usually precedes breakfast. Cabin cleanup usually follows. Younger campers require assistance in keeping personal gear and the cabin

Here They Come!

in good order. A daily inspection with honor accorded the cleanest cabin helps motivate campers. One camp created the Clean Clem award for the best cabin, the Dirty Gertie award for the poorest. This was appreciated by everyone, except the Gertrudes and Clemens who happened to attend camp.

Juniors often need reminders about personal grooming. Some boys will return home in the clothes they wore to camp if you are not alert. Counselors of girls will find good use for a spare hairbrush. Inspect younger campers for personal cleanliness. Mention the purpose of soap, water, and toothbrush. Of course, no camper is permitted to sleep in his clothes, but do not be surprised if a camper refuses to undress. Allow him the dignity of putting on his pajamas after lights-out.

When counseling young campers, check all beds in an inconspicuous manner. Emotional stresses and unrestricted access to canteen beverages may result in wet beds even among campers not normally troubled. Again, guard the dignity of the camper as much as possible. Wet bedding and night clothing must be washed. Chronic bed-wetters should be supplied a moisture-proof mattress cover.

Between the rising bell and lights-out you will be responsible for several cabin activities. Cultivate good cabin etiquette to provide a happy mood. It's hard to enjoy any part of camp if a cabinmate left a muddy footprint in the middle of your cot. Each camper's bunk is his castle, though younger campers may need occasional reminders to tidy their castles.

Since cabins tend to become overcrowded, only personal effects should be stored inside. Athletic gear, clotheslines, hiking sticks, and all livestock belong outdoors. Livestock includes mice, frogs, turtles, lizzards, tadpoles, and snakes. Be sure the clothesline is safely located away from travel routes and well above head level. A low-hanging line can be lethal to a camper dashing through the darkness.

Accidents in and around the cabin usually result from carelessness or horseplay. Teach respect for camp property. Rafters are not for climbing and beds should never be walked on, truths young campers may not have discovered. While these matters may appear obvious, the counselor's presence is the best antidote for cabin mischief that could result in damage or injury.

Cabin Devotions

Cabin devotions can be among the most meaningful parts of camp life, or they can be miserable exercises in endurance. Your camp may supply devotional guides correlated with other teaching and worship content. I wish more camps would adopt this practice. But often you will be expected to prepare your own cabin devotions.

The three basic ingredients for good cabin devotions are Scripture, prayer, and sharing. The lecture simply has no place. Select a brief Bible portion, preferably correlated with the chapel service or Bible study class. Remember, there is a difference in purpose between Bible class and devotions. Avoid using cabin devotions as a time for reviewing memory verses. Attention lags when several campers struggle through half-memorized passages. You might, however, select a memory verse as the Scripture for cabin devotions and quote it in unison with your campers.

Here They Come!

Devotion time should be camper centered. Prayer interests may be shared, then assigned to individuals. You may devise a method for establishing prayer partners within the group. Try "prayer chips," writing each camper's name on a chip of wood and allowing campers to draw partners. Praying around the circle should be practiced only when you are certain all campers are comfortable praying aloud. Introduce conversational prayer, and don't hesitate to remind campers that long-winded prayers are best practiced in private.

Sharing is the key to effective group devotions. Without participation, the exercise does not really become devotions. When the maturity level permits, encourage campers to lead. Use them to read the Scripture. You may wish to divide into smaller groups for prayer. The word discussion frightens some people, so I prefer the word sharing. Any time a camper talks in the group, he is sharing, for better or worse. Real sharing is more than a glib testimony. To share means to take what is yours and give it to another. Encourage expression of familiar, simple things in nontheological language. And fight the urge to sermonize on each camper's contribution!

Several years ago I developed a pattern for devotions to meet the special demands of trail camping. I selected one Bible story or passage for each day. In the morning we explored it, asking ourselves, "What does God say to us today from this passage?" We tried to help campers discover truth, rather than telling them what we thought the passage said.

Thoughts expressed in morning Bible explorations were reinforced during personal devotions right after lunch, called Reflection Time. We encouraged campers to pray the Bible teachings back to the Lord, claiming them personally. Then around the evening campfire, we returned to the same Bible portion, and shared the day's discoveries with each other.

This pattern could be adapted for cabin devotions, particularly when Bible studies take place in the cabin group. Whatever system you develop, strive for maximum participation by your campers, for young campers grow when they share their faith.

Equal in challenge to building group devotions is helping campers develop a meaningful personal quiet time. The after-lunch rest hour offers the best hope for success. Your example will be the best motivation for campers. Suggest a simple pattern: Bible reading, meditation, and prayer. If the camp does not supply a quiet-time guide, allow your campers to help put one together.

Cabin Duty

Many camps have abandoned work details which once formed a normal part of camp life, such as dining hall cleanup and dishwashing. Probably this is for the best. Cabin cleanup remains a significant daily chore, however, and we have already alluded to Clean Clem and Dirty Gertie.

Organize your group so that necessary work is shared equally. A duty roster posted in the cabin allows campers to plan their day and also helps you know whom to look for when some work isn't done. Some of the pain of work is removed if you allow the campers to help draw up the duty roster. Create a sense of pride in your cabin appear-

Here They Come! 65

ance. You may discover opportunities for service projects that can help build cabin pride. Beach cleanup, marking athletic fields, cleaning and marking nature trails, planting trees, building stone retaining walls; any useful work to improve or beautify the camp can build camper interest. Projects should not be too demanding, however, and always carefully supervised. Consult your camp director for instructions.

Your function as a counselor is to relate the camper to the total camp program. Avoid any activity not approved by the camp director which might create jealousy among other campers. Treating your campers to a secret party, which never remains a secret, is unfair to the counselor who may lack the money to treat his cabin. If your camp includes a cabin party night in the schedule, fine, but such a plan should be worked out and financed by the campers within prescribed limits.

Athletic competition between cabins does not always strengthen the overall camp spirit, since cabin groups seldom enjoy balance in strength or skill. A representative from each cabin may compete in an all-camp event, when the opportunity for winning is reasonably equal; a pie-eating contest, for example.

Cabin groups may be encouraged to go on hikes, cookouts, campouts or field trips. If you plan an outing, check each camper to make certain nothing is forgotten, and pace the activity to the capabilities of your group. Outings are for fun, not for hurting. Campouts and nature activity will be discussed in chapter five.

Sooner or later, the time comes for stunt night. Monitor your campers' plans carefully to make sure their selection is in good taste and not threatening to any cabinmate or camp leader. And make certain someone is coordinating the whole program. What could be more demoralizing than to discover Mohawk Cabin performing your skit before your turn comes?

Several sources for skits and stunts are listed in the bibliography, but if you can stir your campers' creative juices, they may think up something original or give a tired old skit a refreshing twist. Simple, brief skits come across more effectively than complex dramas. Use as many of your campers as possible.

Cabin Discipline

The first camp I attended as a boy developed a solution for the problem of restless campers. It was a scout camp, and we were somewhat awed by the uniformed adult and youth leaders. When taps sounded, quiet reigned. Almost. A low murmur that ended soon brought no wrath. Even a snicker was tolerated. But persistent disturbance from one or more in a cabin meant swift judgment, usually for the whole cabin.

With no regard for justice, we were marched out onto the gravel path for an exercise known as squad walking. We marched barefoot the length of the camp and back, a distance of several blocks, without a sound. Some patrols required several trips before utter silence was achieved. We knew this to be cruel and inhumane treatment, but I suppose secretly we felt honored by such attention. Seldom did a cabin require more than one treatment.

I don't generally recommend such discipline, though it proved effective. I do believe leadership should exercise

Here They Come!

authority and discipline chronic offenders. The best antidote to restlessness is tiredness. Keep your campers going full steam all day and close the evening with pleasant, quiet activity. And by all means deny the cabin noisemaker the luxury of an afternoon nap beyond the scheduled rest hour!

Often one or two campers create nighttime problems, and you may find it necessary to deal with them through disciplinary channels. If most campers find sleep difficult to gain, something is wrong with the schedule. The problem usually decreases as the week wears on. A rule demanding utter silence at the bell is both ill advised and unenforceable.

Discipline should not be viewed as an ugly word. In spite of the best programs and the finest plans, some campers will create disturbances. Often you can immediately spot potential trouble in a camper's attitude, but don't write off such a person. Bear in mind that troublesome campers most need the camp. Give your best effort to cultivating friendship with aggressive cabin members. I visited an elderly couple in the home church of a dignified, austere denominational leader. "You should have known him when he was a camper," said the old man. "He was a holy terror!" This can be said of many Christian leaders. The same qualities that enable an adolescent to organize his cabin into a reign of terror for the counselor can later propel him into leadership. But remember that there's a difference between wholesome pranks and malicious conduct.

If the camp is properly organized, you will know the discipline limits within which you operate, and you can explain these limits to your campers. Those who persistently create trouble must be disciplined, and they should know in advance the action they can expect. Except for verbal sparring which never seems to end, avoid disciplining campers in the presence of others. This is probably what they want. A quiet, private talk is more effective.

Your responsibility seldom goes beyond this. Refer problem campers to the head counselor or to another staff member assigned to this task. Explain to the camper that rules require this. Except for deeply disturbed youngsters, the prospect of a confrontation with an adult away from the security of the peer group is frightening. Kinds and degrees of punishment should be worked out by the camp management and applied equally to all campers. Leniency in one cabin and severity in another damages the camp spirit.

Never allow behavior to become an emotional contest between you and a camper. You may win a grudging apology or conformity, but you haven't won the camper. There is no magic formula in disciplining. You can only meet problems as they arise. I don't really know why some adults can master a group of children, while others completely collapse. But if you lack the qualities to command a respectful hearing, you probably shouldn't be a counselor.

I discover my difficulties run in inverse proportion to my degree of preparation. When I am enthusiastic and ready, most campers come along. Since I am not upset by struggling with ill-prepared materials, I am at ease to handle an occasional attention lapse.

Prepare carefully for your ministry of leading your

Here They Come! 69

group. Campers who enjoy cabin life enter the total camp program with a receptive spirit, but trouble in the cabin casts a pall over the whole camp day.

STUDY GUIDE

1. Describe the general characteristics of the age group you will serve at camp, and list their special needs growing out of those characteristics.
2. What approach would you suggest for resolving borderline issues with campers when no clear directive or tradition applies?
3. Why is frequent contact with your campers throughout the day important?
4. The chapter uses the phrase "a camper's moment of discovery." What implications does this have for the counselor?
5. Why do campers need the presence of counselors in all-camp meetings?
6. Suggest methods you would apply to maintain order following lights-out in the cabin.
7. What are some of the elements of good cabin etiquette?
8. List the three parts of cabin devotions and suggest ways you can involve campers.
9. Outline a plan for cabin devotions you feel would be effective.
10. Discuss the values of the discipleship pattern suggested in the chapter.

4

All Together Now

LIKE ANY FIELD OF INTEREST, camping has its philosophers. If you want to stir up action, toss in the words *centralized* and *decentralized*. They will unleash a couple of decades of argument; and, like predestination versus free will, no solution will likely be forthcoming.

The centralized thinker will point out the strength of large-group activity led by skilled specialists: the master teacher-preacher, the super craft director, etc. He will argue that Christian camping existed for 125 years before the decentralized boys came along, and he will hint darkly that doing away with all-camp meetings threatens orthodoxy.

When the decentralized champion gets his turn, he will claim that mass meetings, for all their traditional glory, limit contact on a person-to-person basis. He may cite New Testament examples to show how Jesus and the apostles worked one-to-one and in small groups. He will argue that small-group activity provides for more participation by the camper, hence, better learning.

The centralized defender asks, "And where do you get all those talented small-group leaders? What about the one with three strengths and four weaknesses?" And Mr.

All Together Now

Decentralized counters, "How do you compensate for the introverted camper who loses himself in the crowd?"

While the argument rages, Christian camping moves forward, a blend of both schools of thought. As far as I can determine, there never has been a purely decentralized camp, except for wilderness trips where the small group makes up the total camp. And there really never has been a purely centralized camp, even in pioneer camp-meeting times. The cabin group then was the family, with mother and father as cocounselors.

Today we find most camps operating on a modified centralized plan; some all-camp programming, but with emphasis on the cabin group led by a strong counselor. This combines the strengths of both approaches to camping and provides broad opportunities to serve.

We have looked at cabin-group activities. Now we will consider the all-camp programs. Camps follow several patterns, and your instructions will identify which one you should prepare for. You may be assigned a skill or craft which you will direct for the entire camp. This obviously limits contact with your campers during that time.

Other camps require the counselor to draw up a schedule with his campers for the week, leading them through various activities day by day. This is closer to the classic decentralized approach and has great values. Or you may have no specific assignment, freeing you to serve as you discover needs. In this case, you will relate to your campers however you can to help them gain maximum value from the day.

Practically every Christian camp offers two daily activities that bring all campers together: mealtime and worship.

Morning, Noon, and Night

Recently I visited a camp serving 150 junior boys and girls. The program was excellent until we gathered for lunch. Then the campers degenerated into barbarians, and the counselors weren't much better. There was raucous laughter, playing with food, reaching across the table, and frequent spills. I suggested to one leader that the noise level was intolerable. He yelled, "This is camp!"

That was my point exactly. Since this was a Christian camp, I wondered why kids should be acting like hoodlums. Good manners surely belong within the pale of Christian doctrine! The conduct I observed was boorish and inexcusable. Hopefully the camp you serve will be proud of its mealtime atmosphere. Campers will enter the dining hall in orderly fashion, accepting their food with gratitude and respect. I have shared more pleasant camp meals than the above-described kind. It's all a matter of leadership.

Some camps allow random seating for meals, encouraging cabin groups to mix. Counselors are placed halfway down the table rather than at one end permitting greater ease in maintaining order. Each table becomes an island of pleasant conversation with *please* and *thank you* punctuating requests. Too idealistic? Not when the value of mealtime is recognized.

Where family-style service is practiced, some campers will need help with the size of portions so that the dish serves everyone at the table. Requiring that campers eat a

All Together Now

little of everything, including foods they do not like, is unkind. Camp is no place to try to alter lifelong tastes in food.

Campers should be expected to eat what they take and make no complaints about what they do not like. Watch for the camper who eats little except desserts, then fills up on goodies from the canteen. Ordinarily the canteen is not opened after mealtime except for nonfood items.

Listless eaters may be ill. Alert the camp nurse to any you suspect may not be eating properly. Balanced, satisfying meals ward off most common health complaints, and wise leaders know that good food is the camp's best promotional expenditure.

Occasionally you will find an epidemic of appetite-destroying comments or stories springing up around the table. You will eliminate these, along with food-wasting pranks. Campers who create undue disturbance should quietly be corrected, but not by a counselor bellowing from the far end of the table. It is a general rule that campers will act as rowdy as leaders permit, and where mealtime is bedlam, leaders must assume the blame.

Many camps recognize the hand-raised signal for quiet. The public address system, where one is needed, is kept at minimum volume, never turned up to outshout the campers. Background music is mainly a nuisance in camp. The finest music is the happy murmur of relaxed campers enjoying the fellowship around the table, a primary exercise in Christian fellowship.

Mealtime provides opportunity for several lighter activities: fun songs, mail call, awards and special recognitions, *brief* announcements, introductions. Keep after-meal programs short and sweet. The dining hall crew must begin preparations for the next meal.

All-Camp Meetings

Most camps offer one or more all-camp meetings each day for worship, evangelism, missionary presentations, or Bible study. You can help make these meetings a rewarding experience rather than a battle of wits between leader and camper. Ultimately, the program bears the responsibility for maintaining camper interest, but your presence will help. A dozen counselors warming the back row has little value. Scattered among the campers, the same counselors spread serenity, particularly when a counselor invites himself to sit next to a chronic disturber. Interested, participating counselors beget attentive chapel worship.

Your presence in chapel has other values. Knowing what your campers are learning provides points of contact for cabin devotions and personal counsel. If you have the privilege of teaching a cabin Bible study, you can relate your study to other camp teaching.

As you share group worship, you will want to be alert for spiritual responses among campers. Some who will not respond in traditional ways will betray concern by facial expression. You may find them open to conversation following the meeting. Campfires often offer opportunities for helping campers make spiritual discoveries. Something about the outdoor campfire and the darkness knits campers and leaders together. Today's world offers precious few such moments.

Your role during all-camp programs is to help campers

gain maximum value from whatever activity is available. Nowhere is the counselor more important than during all-camp worship and Bible study.

BEACH, BALL FIELD, AND CRAFTS

Recreation and free periods create varied opportunities for service. Your cabin group demands first loyalty. Is there a boy or girl who needs encouragement? Perhaps a shy youngster longs for a boat ride, but he doesn't qualify unless a counselor goes along. Simple crafts look bewildering to young campers. You can minister to your campers in many ways.

But is this ministering? Are genuine spiritual values found in boats and camp crafts? Consider the counselor who lost his temper when the umpire called him out on strikes. Some dramatic teaching took place concerning the spiritual grace of sportsmanship, though on the negative side! Another counselor comforted a boy who had dropped a fly ball thus losing the game for his team. That moment of comfort was a lesson in Christian love the boy will never forget. Many a camper remembers an afternoon when his counselor quietly shared the wonders of God's love as they sat together braiding a lanyard. Whenever you touch the life of a camper, you minister. God's Spirit may speak to an individual at any moment of the day or night.

Sharing in all-camp recreation periods also adds a safety factor to camp. Swimming is quite safe when a sufficient number of mature persons are on hand to aid the lifeguard. Boating, canoeing, sailing—whenever campers are on the water, great care must be exercised. Dangerous horseplay is minimized when adults are on the scene. While you help your campers explore camp adventures, you help keep them safe.

The degree of emphasis on competitive sports varies according to camp traditions and campers' ages. Everyone who wishes to play should be encouraged, but reluctant participants should not be forced. Proper rules and techniques should be taught. Serving a volleyball looks simple, but remember the first time you tried?

The rifle and archery range attract wide camper interest, requiring experienced leadership both to maintain safety and to teach the skills. Random shooting is never permitted, nor are campers ever allowed on the ranges without supervision. Safety must constantly be stressed in all activity. A flying baseball bat is potentially as deadly as an arrow. You help keep camp safe by mingling with your campers.

You should not feel hesitant to participate in an activity where you are not skilled. Beating the counselor in a game is exhilarating to a camper and not the least bit harmful to the camper-counselor relationship. It helps a camper to discover that adults sometimes lose.

As camps develop more diversified programs, you will find many opportunities to become a learner with your campers. Several nonathletic activities for campers with special interests have been established: drama, photography, the arts, music. You can help your campers grow through new experiences, and perhaps grow yourself.

I have been disturbed to note how many camps fail to properly mark playing fields. While a choose-up ball game in a pasture with stumps and anthills for bases can be de-

All Together Now

lightful, you can forestall many arguments with a sack of lime and a measuring tape. The appropriate dimensions for popular fields are printed at the end of this chapter as a guide should you find it necessary to assist the recreation director.

THE MOMENTS BETWEEN

Elective approaches to camp programming are becoming more common. What do you do when a camper elects to do nothing? We are learning that some young people want time to think, that idleness is not necessarily an evidence of indifference. Quiet, serious-minded campers tend to be neglected in favor of the outgoing camper who drags the counselor off to the rifle range. Watch for the camper who seems uninvolved, but don't force activity when the camper's desire may be time to think.

Often tensions between campers develop in the moments between activities. Waiting for meals produces more than the usual share of squabbles, and is a good time to make your presence felt.

Remember that God works all the time, not just after chapel or campfire. Deeper concerns burn in young hearts than many adults realize. As a counselor you will have the privilege of sharing sacred moments if you keep alert and sensitive to campers' moods. Maintain an open, approachable spirit throughout the day.

STUDY GUIDE

1. Contrast centralized and decentralized camping philosophies and list the apparent strengths and weaknesses of each.

BASEBALL FIELD

For boys under sixteen years of age, official dimensions are as follows: Distance between bases, 82 feet; home plate to second base, 115 feet, 11½ inches; same distance across diamond from first to third bases; home plate to pitcher's plate, 50 feet. Younger boys often use a 75 foot diamond with pitching distance of 45 feet.

GUIDE FOR MARKING PLAYFIELDS AND COURTS

By permission of *Camping Magazine*.

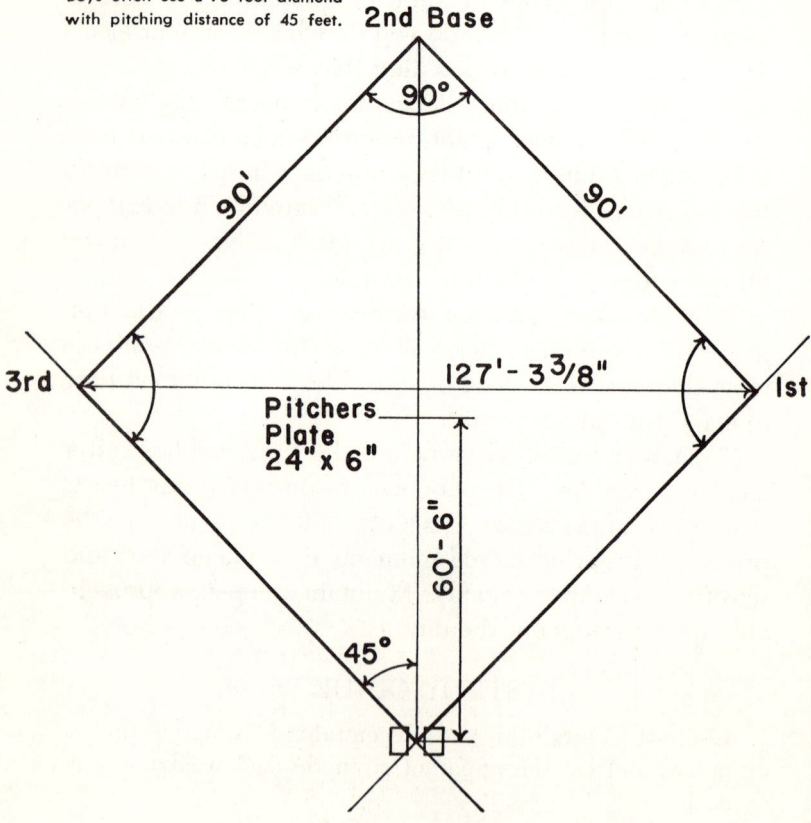

2nd Base

90°

90'   90'

3rd ← 127'-3 3/8" → 1st

Pitchers Plate 24" x 6"

60'-6"

45°

All Together Now 79

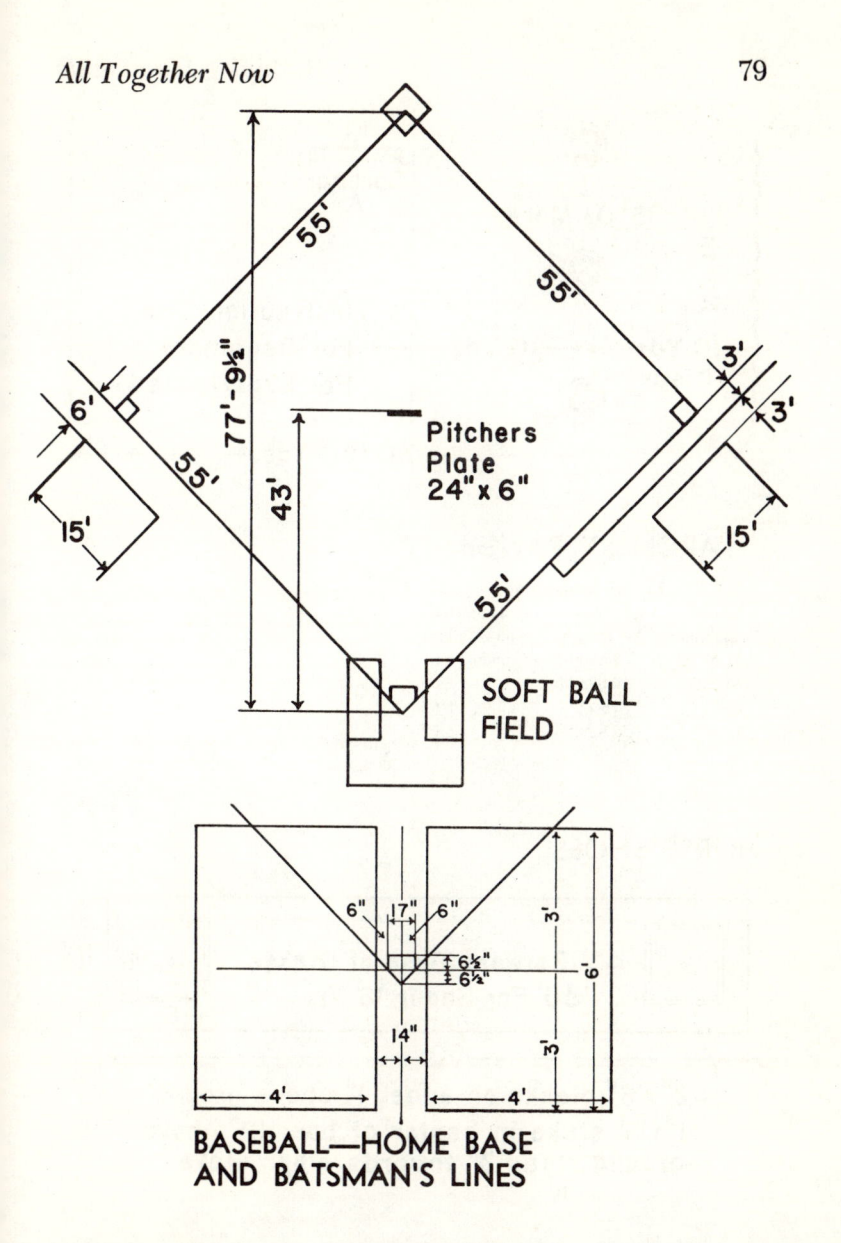

SOFT BALL FIELD

BASEBALL—HOME BASE
AND BATSMAN'S LINES

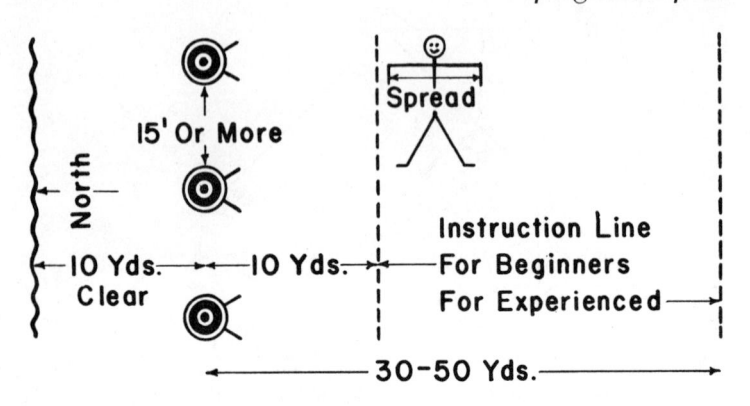

ARCHERY RANGE

Size of Equipment

Spread Measurement	Arrow Length	Suggested Bow Length
57-59"	22-23"	not under 4'6"
63-65"	24-25"	" " 5'0"
69-71"	26-27"	" " 5'6"
75-77"	28-29"	" " 5'9"

HORSE SHOES

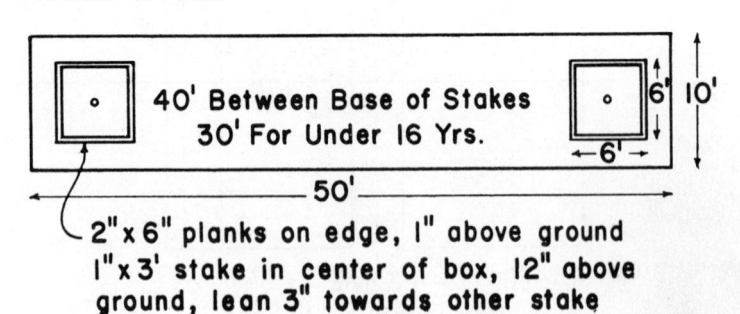

2"x 6" planks on edge, 1" above ground
1"x 3' stake in center of box, 12" above
ground, lean 3" towards other stake

All Together Now 81

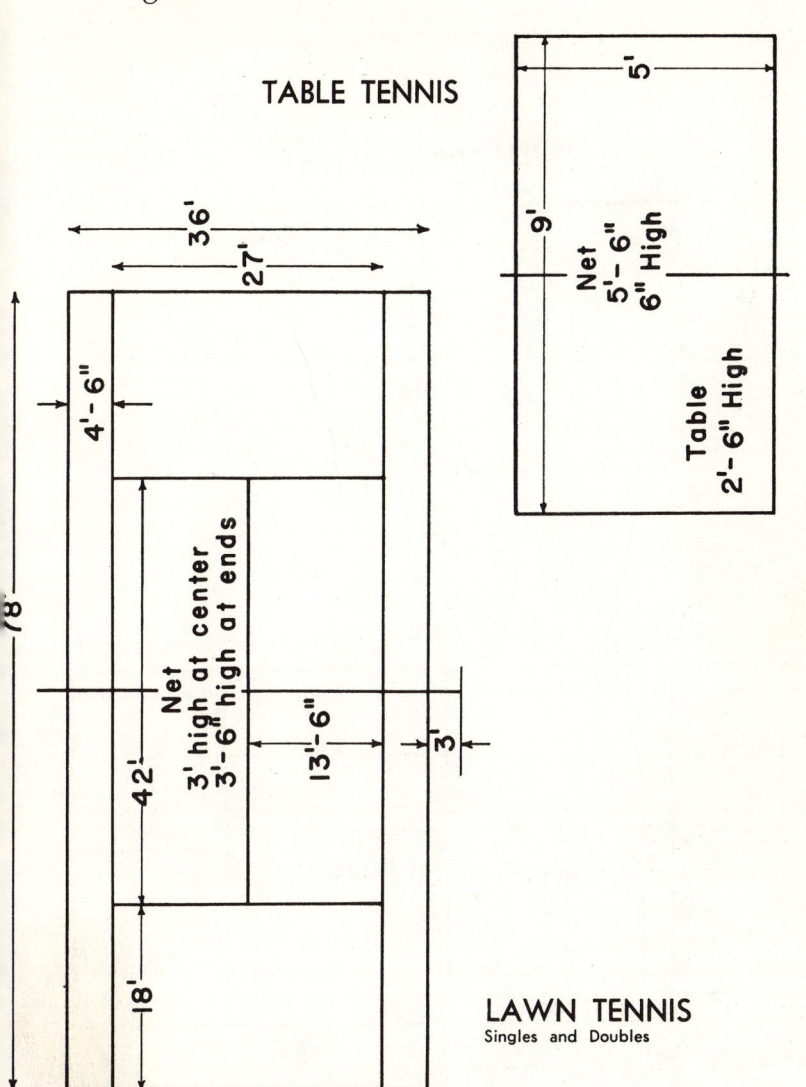

TABLE TENNIS

LAWN TENNIS
Singles and Doubles

VOLLEYBALL COURT

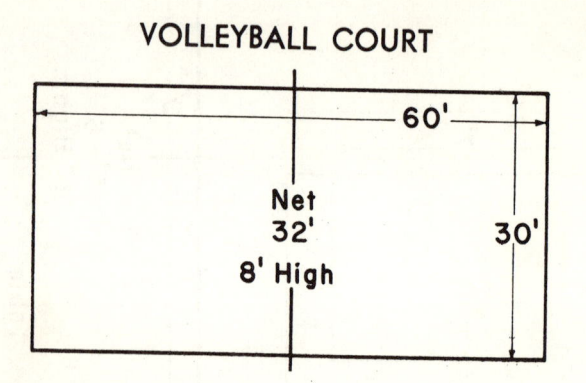

60'
Net
32'
8' High
30'

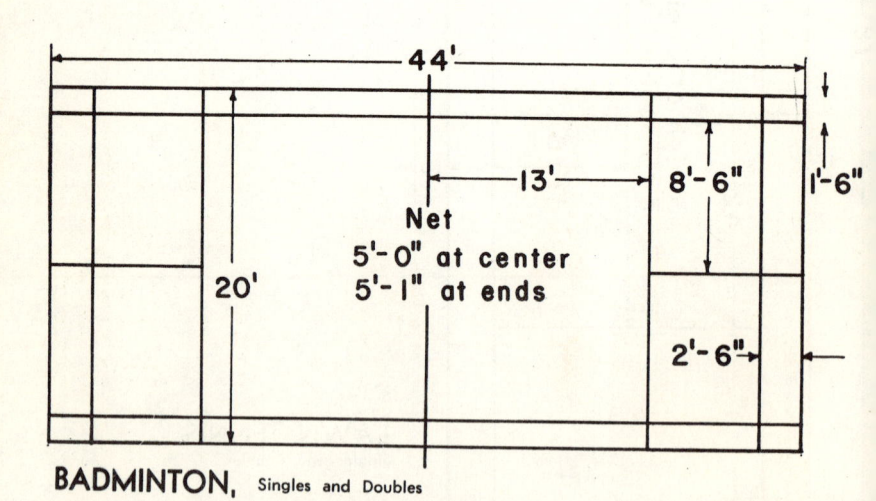

44'
13'   8'-6"   1'-6"
Net
5'-0" at center
5'-1" at ends
20'
2'-6"

BADMINTON, Singles and Doubles

All Together Now 83

BASKETBALL COURT

Standard Court Dimensions

Junior High 42 x 74 feet
High School 50 x 84 feet
College age 50 x 94 feet

Baskets should be 10 feet above ground.
Boys 9 to 11 yrs. of age 40 x 60 feet with baskets 8 feet above ground.
Women's Court 45 x 90 feet
High School Girls 35 x 70 feet

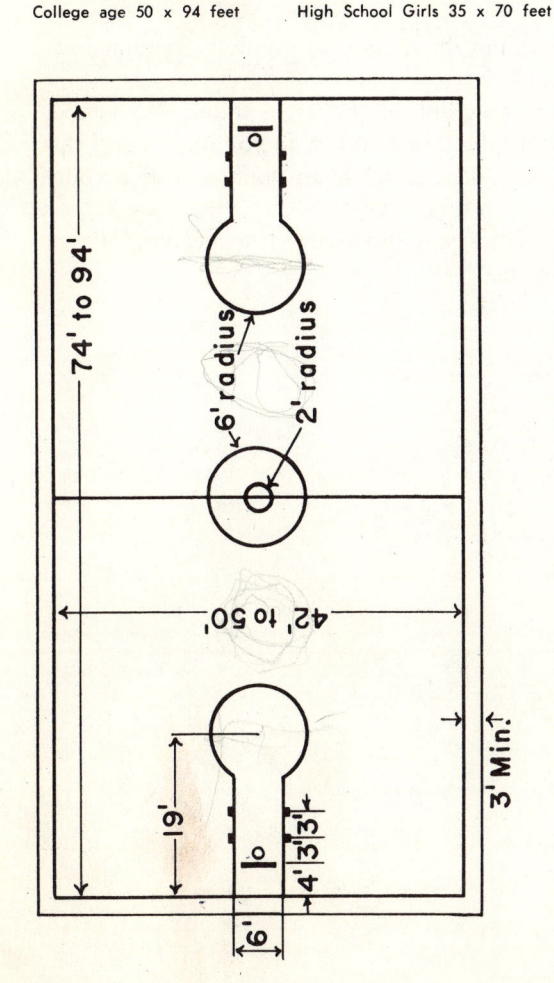

SHUFFLEBOARD

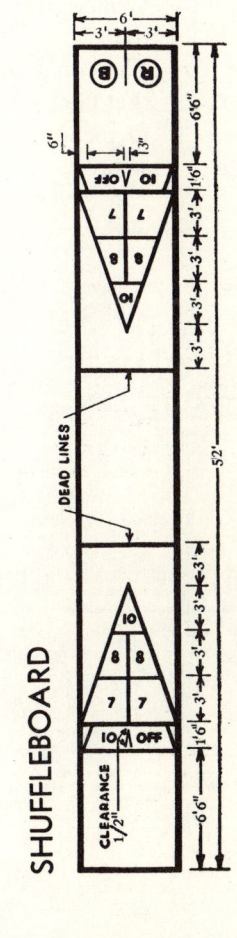

2. How does the modified centralized concept relate to the camp you serve?
3. Suggest several ways the counselor can help maintain a pleasant mealtime atmosphere in the dining hall.
4. Review again the counselor's role in all-camp worship and study.
5. What spiritual values do you see in purely recreational activity?
6. The concluding paragraph of chapter 4 states, "Remember that God works all the time." What do you understand this to mean, and how does it relate to your task as a counselor?
7. List several activities you can share in a meaningful way with your campers.

5

Flora, Fauna, and Dan'l Boone

OLD CAMPER CHARLIE loved to spin yarns about Dan'l and the Boone girls, Flora and Fauna. While his imagination often outstripped fact, Charlie's love for nature and his concern that the pioneer spirit be kindled in young hearts added a rich element to camp life. Camp programs should, as far as possible, be built around activities campers do not ordinarily enjoy at home.

Since most campers come from urban and suburban homes, the camp's natural setting offers a variety of program opportunities. Yet too many camps still limit recreation to the ball field and volleyball court. To be sure, some camps are more suited than others to a nature program, but I never visited a camp yet that did not have trees, sky, birds, and a patch of ground where cookouts and overnights could be held.

CAMP-OUTS AND HIKES

Junior campers do not demand Alaskan wilderness to enjoy outdoor experiences. A circle of tents in the far corner of camp blends with childhood's imagination to provide memorable adventure, especially if the hike to the tent site winds along the lake, through the lush growth of the swamp, along the fence, and finally to the high ground where the tents wait to be pitched. With a little planning, you can lay out a challenging hiking trail on a few acres of land.

But why bother? Surely cabins are more comfortable than tents! Why disrupt the schedule for a silly walk through the woods? That's comfort-loving adult talk. Carried to its logical conclusion, the whole camp idea is a bother. Why not simply haul kids to church and play ball in the parking lot between classes?

Christian camping provides a real-life experience for youth in an outdoor setting where spiritual discovery takes place not only during structured teaching sessions, but through every moment. You have heard many times that salvation is *caught*, not taught. That's why the camp program can offer any activity of interest to campers, and the tradition of Dan'l Boone surely holds interest!

I am encouraged to note the growth of wilderness trips sponsored by Christian camps for older campers. I have more to say about this in another book, *The Wilderness Way*. But there's no reason younger campers should be deprived of wilderness adventure in the camp's backyard, and be taught basic camping skills which will generate interest in greater adventures to come. Building a fire, pitching a tent, paddling a canoe, or riding a horse require about the same skill in any setting. A graduated campcraft achievement program would delight young pioneers.

Nature Discovery

Specialization has come to camp, and the campcraft specialist may assume major responsibility for planning nature

Flora, Fauna, and Dan'l Boone 87

hikes and campouts. But you should be prepared to share adventure with your cabin group. The campfire before bedtime may prove to be the high point of the week, a time of genuine spiritual discovery.

Campouts allow for other kinds of discovery too. Many youngsters know practically nothing about nature; trees, for example. One child reported, "There are two kinds of trees. Christmas trees and the other kind." Campers seldom take kindly to learned lectures on the classification of shrubs and trees complete with Latin nomenclature. But they do appreciate knowing the difference between a cedar and a spruce, between a maple and an aspen. Small markers at eye level along the nature trail will not defile the forest and will enrich the camper's store of nature lore.

I recall a boy staring in awe at the Wyoming skies one night. The stars shone brightly in the moonless night, more stars than the boy imagined there could be. City lights and smog blur the heavens and blur the spirits too. Up there in the mountains all was clear.

Why not familiarize yourself with the major constellations and point them out to your campers? Surely every youngster should know how to locate the North Star. In these days of astronauts and space exploration, the grandeur of the heavens should be taught.

For many years leaders at one camp lamented the presence of a bog which bred mosquitos and took up valuable camp acres. A total waste of land, they felt. Then an imaginative leader came along. He consulted authorities and learned how the bog could be developed into a wetlands nature center with discovery trails and blinds for observing bird life.

Another camp converted a troublesome slough into a small lake, stocking it with pan fish to the campers' delight. Many camps located close to public lands can add hiking and camping to their programs. Campcraft can be taught in any area where small fires can safely be allowed. You will discover that cooking outdoors demands little more than indoor cooking: a secure place for pots and pans, careful control of the heat source, and the proper ingredients in the pot. That's all there is to it. Practice at home over a backyard fire.

Some campers will delight in bird study. Probably more than thirty different kinds of birds frequently visit your camp. Why not create a birds-we-have-seen chart for your cabin or recreation room? But be prepared for early morning hikes if your campers catch the bird-watching bug!

Pioneering Today

Now a word about the pioneering skills and camp kinks which inevitably find their way into camp books. The day has passed for indiscriminate cutting of trees and shrubs for pioneering exercises. Lashing, for example, is a challenging skill but hardly practical today. The woven-twig roaster for broiling fish or steaks which you see pictured in books make far better pictures than cooking utensils. If you don't believe me, try making one that works!

The rule today is never cut a growing shrub or tree or disturb the soil more than is absolutely necessary. This rules out ditching tents (digging a narrow trench along each side for water to drain), a practice which usually fails anyhow. With millions of people using the wilderness each

Flora, Fauna, and Dan'l Boone 89

year, a new conservation philosophy has arisen. In most forest areas the law forbids cutting live growth.

A simple fire grate propped up on stones is superior to the pole between two crotched sticks beloved by campcraft illustrations, though I confess a bent toward building a tripod for hanging pots over the fire when dead poles of proper dimension can be found. Fire holes are nonsense when you think about it. Fire demands oxygen and how do you ventilate a hole? Build the smallest possible fire, digging down to mineral soil for cooking. (Replace the humus and turf after the fire is extinguished. The cooking fire should not serve also as the bonfire, which should be as large as safety permits.)

Today's goal for trail campers requires great care to restore the campsite to its natural state. Even the ashes remaining after the fire is thoroughly soaked and absolutely cold are scattered so that the next camper can scarcely find where the fire had been. This applies of course to camps in areas where permanent fireplaces do not exist.

Garbage, bottles, cans and other leftover debris must not be buried or disposed of in the lake, as was once the custom. Every last vestige of camp life should be completely removed, either by burning or by packing out. Where permanent overnight campsites are used, the woodsmans' code asks that you leave a decent supply of firewood for the next camper, and prop your tent poles and stakes in plain view for the next need.

Practice these principles on all hikes and campouts, even though the camp maintenance truck will be by later. Teach campers to care for their world, and to preserve it for those who will come along later.

Campcraft and nature-lore instruction should never degenerate into an academic exercise. There's hardly a camper alive who wants to attend nature "class." Younger campers will look forward eagerly to a hike, a campout, a cabin cookout or a fishing contest. They will learn by observing and doing. And if there's an award for achievement, most campers will work more diligently.

Camp zoos trouble me, usually because the incarcerated creatures look so unhappy. Why not a gallery of photographs showing animals commonly found near camp. The zoo encourages campers to capture pet frogs, snakes, turtles, and lizards, rendering your life less peaceful.

More animals share the camp than you probably imagine. Rabbits, squirrels, chipmunks, and mice are common sights. Raccoons, skunks, and maybe a black bear may visit during the night. Fox, deer, beaver, muskrats, weasels, and mink make their home in forests, fields, and waterlands near many camps. Since most animals prefer night feeding, campers seldom see them; but their homes and footprints and the evidence of their work can be discovered and identified.

Meanwhile, back at the camp, Marsha and Willie race toward Marsha's counselor.

"It was *so*," pants Marsha.

"It was *not*," Willie insists. "It was too big."

"I saw the yellow mark on its throat, and it was just the right size," Marsha argues.

"Too big," replies Willie.

Miss Counselor produces a brightly-illustrated booklet and Marsha turns triumphantly to the page describing the yellowthroated warbler. *"See?"*

Flora, Fauna, and Dan'l Boone

Willie grudgingly admits defeat, and Marsha gains the honor of entering Bird #27 on the official camp bird roster.

A camper may inform you that there are *millions* of different kinds of insects, a fact you never doubted. He may add that scientists have identified more than 15,000 different kinds of ants and invite you to inspect the official camp anthill just behind the craft building.

Inside the building, you will discover why the campers are alive to nature. Leatherwork and craftstrip still find their place, but your eye is arrested by patterns for simple birdhouses (which houses adorn the trees around camp). A girl sorts leaf specimens preparatory to making spatter prints. Another girl cleverly arranges dried grasses and seedpods into an artistic display.

Lodge and cabin walls are decorated with leaf specimens, insect collections, full-color bird pictures, a great paper-wasp nest, and the handiwork of a beaver. The woodsmanship group discusses conservation, practices proper use of compass and ax. They master a half dozen knots and learn to cook outdoors, with and without utensils. Posters from government forestry and conservation offices create more atmosphere.

Of course the ball field is properly marked out, as are the horseshoe pits and the volleyball court. Campers shoot baskets and play table tennis. Different campers respond to different activities, and whenever campers enjoy themselves in wholesome play, camp is attaining its objectives. Camp must be fun, and part of your task as a counselor is to help your campers enjoy all that camp offers by sharing adventure with them.

References to nature abound in the Bible. Jesus taught

from flowers, rocks, sheep, and rain. David saw the glory of God in the heavens. Read the Sermon on the Mount again, and underline all references to nature. You'll be surprised at the number. Consider the Bible lessons drawn from sparrows, eagles, ants, and the thirst of a deer (hart). If any aspect of camp programming merits special attention, surely nature study qualifies. Considering the rich nature content of the Bible, can we afford to ignore the creation?

You may not share Camper Charlie's love for Dan'l Boone, but you may discover an open door to the heart of many campers through broader use of nature study and campcraft. Who knows what God's Spirit might accomplish in a wilderness corner of the camp?

STUDY GUIDE

1. How is it possible to offer woodlore and campcraft adventures for young campers on a camp with limited acreage?
2. Name several nature study activities possible for most camps.
3. Describe the goals for today's wilderness camper, regarding the camping areas he uses.
4. Name the animals and other wildlife you can expect to see in many camp areas.
5. Suggest ways the camp can foster interest in nature study.
6. Explore the Sermon on the Mount and list at least 20 references to nature or natural phenomena.
7. Describe a typical cabin group overnight, including preparations you would make.
8. Name five birds, five trees, and five constellations you can identify for your campers.
9. In your opinion, what spiritual values may be found in wilderness camping and nature study?

6

Cloudy in the West

THE OMINOUS NEWS from the weather forecaster declares rain for Thursday. That's picnic day plus the all-camp olympics! Rain may come. Chilly weather may close the waterfront. A heat wave will create other problems. The schedule lies shattered at the counselors' feet.

But weather variations are normal phenomena. Football fans sit through rain, sleet, and snow. October hayrides are usually cold, but who cares? Weather is nothing but a circumstance, not a crippling calamity. There's no use denying that camper morale usually sags as the rain continues to drum on cabin roofs. But almost anyone can lead campers in the sunshine. Foul weather puts you to the test, a test you will flunk if you don't prepare for it.

Preparing begins with your attitude toward rain. If you allow weather to determine your mood, you're doomed to a life of recurring misery, for rain is inevitable. So determine to keep your spirits high, rain or shine!

Most camps stand ready to assist you through preplanned rainy day programs. Indoor recreation areas not needed during sunny days are pressed into service. Perhaps the fireplace is kindled. Table-game tournaments flourish. Impromptu amateur shows are scheduled, or the stunt-skit night is moved up. If adequate planning has been done, rain can be almost fun.

Many activities continue as scheduled with meaningful features added. Chapel and classes meet; meals are served on time, with perhaps a bit of extra programming following. The rained-out campfire may be held inside, with or without a fireplace, followed by hot chocolate or popcorn. But recreation and craft hours remain to be filled, probably through your imagination.

If the temperature has not dropped severely, try a rain hike, even for those without rain gear. I hear a cry of alarm, "They'll catch cold!" Not likely. Colds are caught from people, not rain. Germs cause colds, and a rain hike is quite germ free. A severe chill might have some deleterious effect on the health, though I can muster some forty years of early-season trout fishing to debate the point. A brisk hike in the rain followed by a shower or toweling and a change of clothes can't help but improve camp life. But probably the camp nurse will out-vote me.

Barring cold winds or excessive lightning, there is no reason why campers should not be allowed to swim in the rain. An occasional burst of thunder simply provides sound effects. The camp pastor huddled under a tree lamenting the weather is a more likely target for lightning than swimmers or boaters.

Weather should be viewed as a circumstance, not a calamity. When rain begins during the night, the program may be moved back an hour or more to allow the campers extra sleep time. But be ready for surplus energies when night falls!

The movie and filmstrip projector come in handy when

it rains. Ordinarily camp programming avoids duplication with activity commonly enjoyed at home; but under the proper circumstances, films can provide wholesome diversion.

Write out plans in advance for at least one full day of bad weather. Collect a story or two if you will be serving younger campers. Plan folk singing for older campers. As much as I dislike parlor games, you may find several that will profitably amuse your campers. You might plan to invite a neighbor cabin over for the afternoon.

List topics that will draw discussion from most of your campers. Devise simple games and contests. A golf match can be conducted with the use of paper plates (with holes in the center) inverted at various spots in the cabin. A table tennis or small rubber ball propelled by a narrow board complete the equipment. Even old-fashioned hopscotch is not to be scorned.

The secret for rainy-day success lies in variety. Try to change activities just before interest lags. The grimmest test for counselors comes when the rain persists day after day, as sometimes it will. Then exchange ideas with other leaders. Let campers plan activities. Several books in the bibliography suggest rainy-day programs.

Doctor in the Crowd?

Problems other than rain can shatter camp morale for the individual, the cabin group, or the whole camp. Enjoying camp depends largely upon feeling well. As a counselor, your campers' health is of prime concern. Illness takes many forms. **Hurt feelings** can be as painful as a stomach-ache, perhaps more so. Few aches exceed the pain of homesickness. And don't ignore the lovesick!

Never ignore an injury or complaint of pain. Let the camp nurse determine the seriousness of the problem. Do not apply a bandage or administer an aspirin without the nurse's supervision, unless you are away from camp on an extended outing. Take injured or ill campers to the nurse personally, or place them under the custody of a responsible staff person. Let the nurse remove slivers and drain blisters.

Keep alert to symptoms of illness. Nausea, dizziness, stomach pain, headaches, loss of appetite, flushed face, paleness, lethargy, short temper. Any persistent irregularity in appearance or conduct calls for consultation with the nurse.

Never leave an ill camper alone. The camp infirmary accommodates campers who need special care. Never excuse a camper from meals or activity on the grounds of illness. Insist that the nurse make this decision. While serious camp illnesses are not common, you share the responsibility for maintaining health standards.

A knowledge of first aid will prove valuable if the nurse is not readily available, or if you are away from camp on an outing. An injured camper should not be moved until professional help has come, unless it is necessary to save his life. Mouth-to-mouth artificial respiration should be mastered as the best method for reviving victims where breathing has stopped. Severe arterial bleeding must be arrested and breathing restored or death quickly ensues, but most other conditions can wait the arrival of medical help.

Unless there is reason not to alter an injured person's position, ease him onto a blanket or coat and keep him lying down, his head slightly lower than his body, his feet elevated twelve to eighteen inches. Keep him warm, though avoid overheating. Allow him to drink if he is conscious. Reassure him that help is coming and keep curious onlookers away.

Persons injured in diving accidents should be removed from the water on a flat, rigid surface only, since vertebrae may have been damaged and improper handling can paralyze or kill the victim. Watch for shock in all accidents. Shock can kill, even when injury is minor.

Review camp health policies. Check your campers for regular bowel movements. Remind them that all medications should be administered by the nurse, even those they bring with them from home. Immediately report all injuries no matter how slight to protect the health of the camper and the camp.

The Homesick

Young boys and girls often experience homesickness. Most recover and stay through the week, but a few cannot master their illness. And it is a genuine illness, though of psychological origin. As far as I know, it has never been fatal. Ridiculing the homesick is heartless and futile, but yielding to the camper's wish to go home is not always best. Homesickness grows out of insecurity and fear; but sooner or later a child must learn to survive away from parents and home, so you will do him a favor if you can help him stay in camp.

Suggest some area of unusual interest, a horseback ride,

for example. Assure the camper that homesickness happens to most people and that it will go away. Avoid a phone call home if at all possible; the mother may be suffering child sickness, and both will end up bawling!

Enlist the help of a woman staff member for a homesick boy, and try to resolve the problem before nightfall. Homesickness is highly contagious! Darkness intensifies loneliness, and a child crying in the cabin can unnerve marginal cases. You might have quite a night!

Make it seem difficult for the child to be released from camp. As a last resort, allow him to phone home with the information that his parents will have to arrange travel. If there is no relief, you will simply have to allow him to leave. An incurably homesick child can become physically ill. Even though this may not happen, camp will be a week-long nightmare, a memory of horror for life.

Offer love and affection, and commend the homesick to the loving Saviour. Homesickness to a little camper is about as bad an illness as he can know.

The Lovesick

You may have to deal with a love-sick junior or young adolescent camper. This transient surge of emotion often fastens on an unsuspecting adult, perhaps you. You may find this note tucked under your pillow:

> Dear ———,
>
> You are the most wonderful person in the whole world, and I love you with all my heart. I know you don't care for me, or even know I exist, but I love you anyway. When you smiled at me this morning, I

thought my heart would explode. Please don't tell anyone. Love and kisses.

Usually the note will not be signed, but eventually the writer will make himself known. Lovesickness seems to afflict girls more often than boys, or perhaps girls are more expressive. At any rate, the condition exists. Though childhood crushes are shortlived and usually harmless, they are very real. In spite of every caution not to tamper with the mysterious emotional moods of childhood, the problem must be met when it arises. When you discover one of your campers smitten by another staff person, be careful not to display amusement. Let the camper know that such feelings are common, and that the person they admire is fortunate to be loved. But gently remind the child that these feelings will change in a day or so.

When you are the object of the crush, the problem is a bit more delicate. You might say something like, "Thank you, Carol (or Johnnie). That was one of the nicest notes I ever got. I'm very happy to have you for one of my best friends. We're going to have a wonderful time in camp this week."

The emotions of a child must be honored, though any response that would encourage the love feelings is cruel. Never laugh at such a camper, or betray the incident to others who might in turn show ridicule. The crush will soon pass, but not the hurt if a confidence is betrayed. If the crush persists, refer the camper to the camp nurse or pastor, someone of the same sex. While pointing out to the afflicted that leaders like all campers equally, you must seek to preserve the dignity of the camper with kindness and understanding.

Mary Loves Joe

Love affairs in co-ed teen camps must be approached with a wholesome point of view. It is both normal and desirable for young people to discover an increasing interest in the opposite sex. Leaders continue to debate the comparative values of one-sex versus co-ed camps. The pattern in many places finds co-ed camping beginning at the high school level while other camps operate co-ed programs from junior age on up. Several excellent camps serve older boys in specialized camping ministries with no apparent lack of interest because girls are absent. All-girl camps also report good results, particularly in trail-camping programs.

The mood of our day and the moral climate of many communities make co-ed camp leaders increasingly aware of incipient dangers. Prospective campers should understand clearly the social standards of Christian camping, and those who cannot accept the standards should be encouraged to stay home.

Should Christian camping accept open courtship as normal social responses among high school campers? Not in my opinion. Warm friendships, wholesome affection, and companionship do not dilute the spiritual atmosphere. But counselors should pass the word quietly and firmly when acceptable standards are violated.

Some camp leaders play up boy-girl interests in a childish fashion which is demeaning to the campers. This occurs most often in junior high camps where the campers already lack sufficient maturity to relate to one another in a meaningful way. Silly allusions to romance only magnify the problem.

Cloudy in the West

Helping campers accept their God-given sexuality and integrate this life-force into their Christian experience is one of camping's great ministries. Openness and honesty with campers will accomplish far more than impossible rules. Overt violators of good taste should be approached by camp leaders with kind but firm alternatives. Accept the camp standards or go home. Sometimes staff members must be reminded to exercise self-discipline too!

Tragedy

Dark clouds of tragedy can destroy a camp more quickly than rain, yet tragedy is possible whenever people engage in the kinds of activity found in camp. Morality as well as the law require adequate standards for health and safety in all camp programs. Even where trained, responsible leadership is provided tragedy may strike.

The amazing fact is that few deaths or major injuries occur in Christian camps in spite of the millions of campers who participate each year. But one death is too many, if that death resulted from carelessness. Negligence has cost some camps their property and left lifetime scars on the conscience of leaders.

Should a death or serious injury occur, the counselor should not communicate with anyone beyond securing help. The camp director is the spokesman for the camp, and he will make a full report of the accident. You will report to him your involvement, supplying names of witnesses and every known factor. Do not attempt to speak for the camp to authorities or bystanders.

Campers should be removed immediately from an accident scene. Tragedy is loaded with peril, for mass hysteria can sweep through the camp. It is best to deal with campers in cabin groups rather than in a general assembly. Then as soon as possible resume normal camp activity. This in no way shows disrespect for the victim.

Direct conversation away from the accident and avoid speculation. Facts should be frankly shared, and the gravity of the accident truthfully reported. When a death has occurred, the cause should be explained clearly as soon as it is known. But accusations or blame-fixing must not be allowed.

A brief, comforting reading of Scripture and prayer will soothe fears. Camp should rarely be closed because of tragedy unless the event completely devastates camp morale, for no good cause can be served. It is the director's duty to notify the parents of an accident victim and determine adjustments in camp schedules.

Above all, shun the temptation to rationalize tragedy by suggesting that God allowed it to happen for some spiritual purpose. Campers may indeed be moved to make decisions because of the tragedy, but to excuse a death on that premise is ignoble. Most camp leaders serve a lifetime without this sad experience, but tragedy can strike at any time. Prepare yourself in prayer for such an eventuality, and be ready to stand by your campers.

EVACUATION, SEARCH, AND RESCUE

Some camps have worked out evacuation procedures, should any circumstance make it necessary to move campers out in a hurry. Forest fires, floods, tornados, even earthquakes in some regions make it vital to have such a plan. All leaders should be aware of the plan and how they

Cloudy in the West

should function when the evacuation decision is made. While the need may never arise, adequate preparation could save lives.

Search and rescue plans have been readied for camps in wilderness areas. Ordinarily, campers would not be employed in off-grounds activity, but a search plan covering the camp area can prove vital. A tag left behind on the buddy board by a forgetful camper can give the lifeguard anxious moments. He has no alternative but to assume the person is in the lake. A preplanned search can comb the camp in a matter of minutes, and usually the forgetful camper will be located, even while a search of the swimming area is under way. Brief your campers on their responsibilities for search and rescue. All camps should conduct fire drills in the various buildings where large numbers gather. Review procedures with your campers should a fire break out in the cabin.

Campers should be drilled on the necessity for safety. Most camp tragedies can be traced at least in part to camper carelessness. Parents and churches entrust their young people to camp leaders, assuming they will exercise every possible caution to return the campers safely home. No unnecessary risks should be taken, and prayers should ascend daily for divine protection.

STUDY GUIDE

1. List five rainy-day activities you could lead.
2. What would you do if one of your campers became ill some distance from the dispensary on the camp grounds?
3. What first aid or medications would you dispense while on the campgrounds?

4. Describe briefly the field treatment for shock following injury.
5. What approaches would you take to help a homesick camper?
6. When a camper crush develops toward a staff member, how would you seek to help the camper?
7. How may a wholesome boy-girl relationship be encouraged in a co-ed teen camp?
8. Name several principles involved in handling camp tragedies.
9. What circumstances might arise in the camp you will serve when advance preparation or drills might avert injury or death to campers?

7

May I See You–Alone?

CAMP COUNSELING is more than maintaining order and playing games. The counselor's duties are many and varied, all of them directed toward one goal: fulfilling the objectives of Christian camping in the camper's life. You will attack some responsibilities confidently, others fearfully. But the one responsibility you should determine to master is the art of counseling individuals, for your greatest ministry lies here.

When we attach the word "counseling" to a conversation between two persons, the image arises of an austere office with a couch. This is unfortunate. Counseling is mostly caring and listening. No magic formula exists that will dissolve every personal problem campers bring to camp. Counseling individuals never ceases to be an adventure; and as often as not, you will come from the counseling opportunity unsure of the results. Professional counselors readily confess a meager batting average if success means a complete cure. However, there are principles which enable you to be of some help to most campers and of significant help to many.

THE ANATOMY OF COUNSELING

The two organs most important in counseling are the heart and the ear, in that order. Love and listening. Too many would-be counselors seem to think the brain and the tongue are most important. The most dangerous animal most campers will ever encounter is the eager-beaver, amateur-psychiatrist counselor; the one who has read a few books and taken a course or two in psychology.

Books are fine, and you should read as many as possible. But I hope you will major in the Book, where you'll find more common-sense help in counseling than in all the other texts put together. Jesus loved people and He listened to them. He often met problems with a question. He allowed people to discover their own needs by the response His questions drew forth.

There is no substitute for genuine compassion, which is simply another word for love. Compassion never turns kids off, never half listens, never says, "That reminds me of the time...." Compassion understands that every camper has great potential for good. Compassion accepts mean campers, sullen campers, lying campers, and thieves. Compassion understands that every act has a cause, a cause that may baffle the wrongdoer more than the counselor.

Compassion refuses to be shocked. Campers rarely confess sins that the counselor is not capable of committing and probably has committed in one degree or another. Campers seldom use a word that the counselor has not heard before. Bad books, wicked deeds, hypocrisies, drink, tobacco, drugs, immorality; they are as common as humanity. It's useless to tell an offender simply to quit sinning. Most of them would gladly quit if they could.

May I See You—Alone?

A lad approached me one August morning after camp Bible study. "Can I talk with you, Cap?" We found a quiet corner. He talked about generalities for a while, about the Bible study just ended. Then he got down to his problem. What did I think about a friend of his who pretended to be a Christian, yet he habitually stole?

"What do you steal?" I asked. I tried to speak conversationally. I could see denial building in the boy's eyes as he searched mine. Then he spread his hands in despair. Mostly he stole small parts for his model-car hobby. Even when he had the money in his pocket, he stole. Why?

Stealing is a common crime, probably exceeded only by lying as a sin practiced by Christians. We usually rationalize our stealing and lying into pious oblivion, but this lad had the courage to face his problem and talk about it. He talked for a long time, telling again and again how foolish and petty his thefts were. "Why do I do it?" he asked.

I could only answer, "I don't know." I lacked the training to unravel the complexities of a personality that found it necessary to steal. Certainly it was pointless to tell the boy to quit stealing. He wanted to quit, but how? What he needed was my heart and ear; so I cared and listened and counted it a privilege. After we prayed together, for the boy was a genuine Christian, he said, "Thanks, Cap. You've helped me a lot." I hadn't said ten sentences in an hour.

The healing power of listening has gained prominence lately through a rash of books and articles, but we're slow to practice it. It's easier to talk than to listen. Honest listening demands discipline, both of the brain and the tongue. A counselor must resist the compulsion to interrupt.

Listening is the other end of confession. A mysterious therapy flows out of sharing needs. While the confessional is extrabiblical, confession surely is not. There is little cleansing apart from confession. Effective counseling partakes somewhat of the atmosphere of the confessional; as you listen, you heal. When you have lived among your campers in such a manner that one will share his deepest secrets, you have reached the pinnacle.

Listening is essential, because the real need seldom emerges right away. The camper tests the water with a mild sin to discover how chilly your response will be. If you jump on that problem, you will fail. If you listen with compassion and acceptance, the camper will likely go on, probably still skirting his real burden. He cannot be completely honest until he feels secure. He must be confident that you will not reject him when you learn his most grievous sin.

All of us have a built-in scale of wickedness from gray to black. Your scale may differ from the campers. Furtively puffing a cast-off cigarette may hardly call for penance on your scale, but a junior camper steeped in the antismoking tradition, may feel such a sin to be nearly unpardonable. Never treat a confession lightly. The conscience is a delicate instrument, and quite readily manipulated. Compassion and listening even in matters that seem trivial can bring comfort to a youthful confessor.

Helping Campers Solve Common Needs

So far we have considered counseling in relation to sin

problems. But don't expect a rash of confessions, and don't attempt to precipitate confessions through a contrived pseudosensitivity climate. Campers have been known to vie for the most lurid confession! We glamorize sin by making heroes of great sinners who became converted. It takes as much grace to save a child as a drug addict, only childhood conversions do not make effective posters. Most personal counseling opportunities will relate to fairly simple matters. Some of them will be little more than the camper's desire for personal attention, and there's nothing wrong with that. Make your heart and ear available. That's why you're in camp.

Personal counseling aims at helping campers discover their problems and voluntarily apply a solution. Counseling is not advice-giving. Some situations will suggest an obvious course of action, and you should not hesitate to be directive. Should a camper finish school? Of course! But if he seriously asks that question, you can be almost sure you haven't heard the real problem.

Forcing a response on a camper rarely achieves much good, such as compelling one camper to apologize to another. Mere words mean nothing. Bringing a camper to a point where he sees he has hurt someone so that his apology is sincere, blesses everyone. Most useless is that strange practice of forced public confession. When public confession comes spontaneously everyone gains.

You will discover counseling books that talk about *directive* and *non*directive counseling. The distinction is fairly obvious. Using the Bible wisely permits you to be directive and nondirective at the same time. The more you know your Bible, the better able you will be to help campers find their way. When a camper accepts the authority of Scripture, you have but to help him search the Word. Jesus said, "The Law. What does it say?"

If a camper rejects the authority of the Bible you have another problem, and you must judge when the situation demands directive counseling. Sin is sin no matter what an individual chooses to believe. But unless the camper *voluntarily* accepts your directive, not much is gained. Your purpose is not to win arguments over moral or practical issues but to change lives. Real change is achieved through the spirit of the person who voluntarily accepts change.

In a sense, changing campers is what camp is all about; changing unconverted campers to Christians, changing disobedient Christians to committed Christians, changing the life direction of aimless Christians. All learning involves some change and accomplishing real change is a complicated matter. Don't mistake conformity with change. Many "decisions" are nothing more than bowing to a custom the camper understands to be expected of him. Change originates within, and your best opportunity to achieve change is through person-to-person encounters.

Almost any kind of personal contact is good. Don't hesitate to schedule interviews but don't expect too much from such encounters. If the camp requires written evaluations tell your campers so. Tell them if a copy of the report will be sent to their home churches. The advantages of such an announcement are obvious!

One of the advantages is the necessity for time alone with each camper, even though the counselor-initiated interview is ordinarily the least productive kind. Expect pre-

May I See You—Alone?

meditated responses, the kind a camper thinks will look good on his "report card." But if you obey the heart-ear law for counseling, you can glean valuable insights.

Another personal encounter opportunity, gaining popularity in camps, grows out of achievement programs. Bible memory verses, crafts, nature projects, skills; whatever brings camper and counselor together holds promise for useful exchange. But don't forget to listen!

The traditional evangelistic interview offers the most precious and the most dangerous counseling situation you will face. Any method you may discover that confronts a camper with the biblical provision for personal salvation is worthy, but beware of systems that impose ideas on a camper or put words in his mouth! Let the Holy Spirit work. Someone has said, "We win people, the Holy Spirit wins souls."

Soul-winning is the work of God in the truest sense, and we dare not intrude. We can declare what God has said and what God requires. But beware of imposing assurance on an unsure heart.

I hope the day never comes when evangelistic invitations cease in our camps. While public invitations suitable for older youth and adult audiences require modification for smaller children, campers should be afforded an opportunity to respond to the urgings of the Spirit. You should be prepared to help.

In all learning there is a mysterious moment of acceptance, some blending of mind and will that opens the understanding to a new idea. This is supremely so in the discovery of spiritual truth. Unless God works, nothing happens. Mass appeals demand scrupulous care with children, but every evidence of interest demands personal attention regardless of the age. You become the catalyst, and you never share a more sacred moment nor one more to be coveted, than when a spirit is newborn. Be alert day and night for opportunities to lead campers to Christ, your ultimate experience as a counselor.

A sad remark heard sometimes in evangelistic services goes like this: "We'll sing one more verse, and then the invitation will close." This is blind presumption. Man cannot determine when God will touch a heart, and it is no affront to the preacher if a soul is not prepared to respond at that moment. Christian camping opens unlimited opportunities for evangelistic interviews. I regret the proposition that one hour is more suited for salvation than another.

A wooded trail, a fallen tree, a great rock along the shoreline; wherever the camper may be when that mystic moment of acceptance comes, that is the right time. Do not hesitate to ask a camper concerning the state of his soul. Either he is saved or he isn't. Buy up every opportunity to point campers to Christ, but beware of psychological pressure tactics.

Chart and Compass

The proper use of Scripture in counseling insures lasting benefits. I have stated that quoting "Thou shalt not steal" to a confessed thief has little value and imparts no new information. Having him read 1 John 1:9 offers a base for a new beginning, and opens the way for him to follow in the spirit of Zacchaeus.

The broader your knowledge of the Bible, the greater

May I See You—Alone?

your strength in counseling. One scripture promise relevant to the camper's need is worth more than a dozen psychological explanations. Encourage the camper to read and interpret the verses. Say to the camper, "On the basis of this promise (command) of God, what do you feel you should do?" A course of action may be obvious to you, and probably to the camper also. Your task is to help the camper adopt the course of his own will.

Know Your Limitations

The camp pastor, program director, and head counselor will be prepared to help with problems that tax your experience and skill. Often you will refer a camper who comes to you for help to another staff member for additional counsel.

Occasionally you may find yourself in deeper water than you can tread. "Margie, I wonder if we shouldn't ask the camp pastor (nurse, head counselor) to help us." Gaining Margie's consent, you will take her to the camp pastor, introduce her, then leave. One counselor at a time is the general rule.

Unless you have had training, seek help with complex problems. The intricacies of human personality demand great care lest problems be driven deeper and confusion be multiplied. Ordinarily camper's burdens will be direct and identifiable. Help them make decisions, but don't decide for them.

Problems for Personal Counseling

What kind of problems can you expect campers to bring to you? Probably as many as you have campers. It would be false to suggest that most of your camp day will be spent unraveling tangled young minds. Yet no part of the counselor's work holds more promise for the camper than the problem-facing session.

Troubled campers must conquer mountains before they can freely unburden their hearts. First, they fear loss of status in the counselor's eyes (plus a dread that the counselor might tell others). Second, they often believe their problem is peculiar to themselves, in degree if not in kind, bringing the fear that they are abnormal. Third, they have tried to solve the problem before and failed, suggesting a hopeless weakness.

We have discussed the week-long opportunity for building rapport between counselor and camper and the possibility that a deeply troubled camper will engage in preliminary skirmishes before attacking the real problem. Unless you have known him prior to camp, it is unlikely that time will allow the most troublesome concerns to emerge. When you sense serious problems, encourage the camper to seek help. The average camper will open his heart when he learns that you will not reject him because of his problem. Assure him that his problem is common to many, that it *can* be solved with God's help.

Desire for Salvation

Several printed methods are available to guide you in leading a camper to a decision for salvation. Study them carefully, but use the Bible throughout the counseling session. As in all good counseling, keep the interview camper-centered. Let the camper read a few verses from the Bible, examining them closely. Do not attempt to give a sermon

May I See You—Alone?

on the atonement or expound on total depravity. Allow the Holy Spirit to apply Scripture to the mind and heart; for unless the Holy Spirit is speaking, your words are useless. If the Spirit is speaking, God's Word is enough. No principle of soul winning is more important than this: base the camper's decision on the promise of God.

Do not force a decision, though you may ask questions that require specific answers concerning the meaning of the Bible verses. Many patterns have been used for dealing with salvation. Most of them include the following concepts:

> Everyone needs to be saved.
> Romans 3:23; Isaiah 53:6
>
> There is only one way to be saved.
> John 3:13, 18; Acts 4:12
>
> Jesus saves all who truly believe in Him.
> John 1:12, 3:16, 6:37
>
> Salvation means a new life in Christ.
> Ephesians 2:8-10; Colossians 3:1

Remember the importance of helping the new Christian confess Christ immediately. Treat every decision with dignity and particularly the decision for salvation.

DESIRE FOR SURRENDER

A growing spiritual experience demands new points of beginning. Many Christians can point to crisis experiences following salvation. These experiences can be of great significance to the camper. Many will sense God's leading into a church-related vocation. Again, do not force decisions. Let God speak to hearts. You do a great injustice to a young person when you draw from him a pledge of specific service when the conviction of God is not the motivation in his heart. There is nothing quite so important to a minister or missionary as the certainty that *God* has called him to his task.

The cumulative effect of a good camp program and the absence of many usual distractions heightens the camper's spiritual perception. Jesus Christ may become more real and more dear than the camper imagined possible. Such experiences are to be cherished. You may have the privilege of sharing sacred moments and lending lasting beauty long after the high, holy emotion has passed. Be ready with a bouquet of Bible verses to enrich the hour.

Doubts and Questions

You will learn early in your counseling experience to discern between honest questions and heckling. Youth is an age of doubting, particularly the later teens. How do you know the Bible is God's Word? What about evolution? Can all the millions of non-Christians be lost? How do you know for sure you have true faith? Kindred questions tumble out of young hearts faster than you can gather them. The strongest reply possible is your unswerving faith in God and the Bible, even when you must answer, "I don't know how to answer that question." You know God is true because He is real to you. You know the Bible is God's Word because of its effect in your life.

how can i know god's will?

No question is more critical for sincere young Christians.

May I See You—Alone?

You dare not presume on God's domain. Counsel the camper to be faithful in known duties (Bible reading, prayer, witnessing, personal holiness), and assure him that God will lead in specific needs. Warn him that disobedience in everyday Christian requirements precludes any right to God's leading for life's major callings (Proverbs 3:5-6).

MORAL DIFFICULTIES

Most young people are wrestling with basic virtues. Lying, cheating, stealing, and swearing are accepted as indifferent matters in community and school life. Sexual temptation is aggravated by the particular stage of physical development campers are experiencing, and by the sensual nature of today's magazines and books.

The high moral tone of Christianity is a whip to the tender conscience of sincere young people, many of whom may be gripped by sinful habits before they know the consequences. You will need to teach both God's loving forgiveness and His refusal to countenance sin. Looking around and within may soften your reproach when you hear confessions. While sin is never excused, its presence in young lives can largely be traced to the greed of the adult world. You are part of a Gideon's tiny band rescuing God's people from the oppressor.

A comprehensive listing of problems you will face in counseling is impossible, and no sure formula for problem-solving can be constructed. In every case you will seek to help the camper identify his real problem, evaluate it in the light of Scripture, and help him to take necessary steps to correct the matter.

Under certain circumstances you will recognize the need for old-fashioned directive counseling. Campers need to know that authority exists in the Bible, parents, government, camp rules, and basic laws of health and safety. You are obligated to direct a camper into a proper path when his attitude or deeds threaten danger to himself or others.

Years ago I found myself appointed director for the high school week at a small camp. I was new to the area, and I found the staff fearful as night approached. I discovered the lights-out bell traditionally signalled a riot, with cabin raids, pranks, and boys and girls sneaking off into the darkness.

"Why has it been permitted?" I asked. The best answer I could get was "tradition." Apparently each year the campers sought to outdo their predecessors in creating a dangerous moral climate. On several occasions the campers had literally manhandled adult staff members, throwing them in the lake. Little wonder the attendance was small.

While I'm not particularly heroic, I have a sense of responsibility toward campers and their parents. I proposed a drastic remedy which the staff accepted with skepticism. At the campfire I quietly announced that all campers would be in their cabins at the lights-out bell and remain there until morning. There was a snicker here and there. Then I stated that I would be around shortly after lights-out and require each counselor to report. Any camper absent without valid reason would find his bags packed when he returned, and a phone call would be made immediately to his home requesting his parents to come for him. There were a few sullen stares. We went on with the campfire program and concluded our first camp day peacefully.

May I See You—Alone?

Not one camper ventured from his cabin after hours. I was prepared to follow through, even to closing down the camp, and the campers sensed this. The staff declared it was the best high school camp they could remember.

While camp is for the camper, it must be managed by adults who exercise responsible authority to assure the moral and physical safety of the campers. As you counsel individuals, you will allow campers to discover solutions to their problems and voluntarily adopt remedies. But you will not hesitate to apply "Thus saith the Lord" when the occasion demands.

STUDY GUIDE

1. The heart and the ear are named as symbolic of the two most important elements in counseling individuals. Explain the implications of this for your ministry to campers.
2. "Personal counseling aims at helping campers discover their problems and apply solutions." In your opinion, do you feel this is an adequate goal for counseling? Why?
3. "Counseling is not advice-giving." Is this a true statement? Why do you think it is, or isn't?
4. List several kinds of opportunity for counseling campers individually.
5. What is the best time for counseling campers concerning personal salvation?
6. What steps would you take to help a camper with deep mental or spiritual problems?
7. The chapter names three mountains a camper must overcome before he can really unburden his heart. What are they?
8. Describe your approach when a camper comes desiring to find Christ as Saviour.

9. How would you respond if a camper asked a question that baffled you?
10. Directive and nondirective counseling: what do you understand to be the difference, and when would you become directive?

8

The Heart of the Matter

ONCE THERE WAS A MAN who desperately wanted to cross the sea. Day and night he dreamed of reaching the other shore, but he had no way to cross. One day someone said, "Why don't you build a boat?" The man began, learning the skills and gathering materials. Slowly his boat took shape, and everyone stopped to admire the workmanship. He proved to be an exceptionally fine boat builder. Even as he worked he thought of improvements, and soon he owned the finest boat on the coast. The last I heard he was still improving his boat.

How easily we forget our real goals, a danger camp leaders must constantly face. Christian camping has grown into a powerful instrument for evangelism and Christian education, possessing a breadth and flexibility greater than any other kind of spiritual ministry. This sweeping statement probably will not be challenged. Since camping belongs to everyone, no other work is threatened.

Increasingly the church uses camping as a base for outreach and training, with year-around programs becoming the norm. Retreats, leader planning seminars, weekend family camps, lay training institutes—the variety of needs camp can meet seems endless. But the goal remains constant: to win people for Christ and to train Christians in godliness.

As a camp counselor you fit into the very heart of Christian camping as young people participate in week-long camps. The burden of Christian camping is to help each camper cross the sea toward the shore of spiritual maturity. We have discussed many systems and techniques to help in this crossing, but beware lest you become so absorbed in building the boat you forget the goal!

Aims for the Camper

The goals for Christian camping are identical with those of the church: to fulfill God's purpose in people. While we can talk about evangelism and Christian education as separate concepts, they are in reality two inseparable aspects of God's plan. Evangelism seeks to lead campers to that point where they accept God's gift of salvation. The moment they enter the door of faith, they find themselves in a new life; and the task of Christian education begins.

You might consider Christian camping in the light of Jesus' raising of Lazarus. The Master issued three commands by the graveside that remarkable day, two of them to the friends who stood by and one to the dead man. You can adjust the application any way you wish, but I see the three basic elements of Christian camping in this story in John 11.

We acknowledge that many campers come to us dead in trespasses and sins, to use Paul's phrase from Ephesians 2. They come with all manner of shrouds: lust, falsehood, pride, and sometimes drugs and disease. These are the normal trappings of spiritual death; and the fact that

The Heart of the Matter

campers bring problems to camp, should not dismay leaders.

Christian campers also come in shrouds, problems lingering from days spent in the old nature. Camp would hardly be needed if campers were fully mature. Helping campers find cleansing and release is the grand purpose of camp.

Jesus' first command at Lazarus' grave called for action. "Take away the stone!" Opening a fresh grave offends the sensibilities of man. The odors of death are never pleasant. Surely Jesus could shout through a mountain, and angels could open the grave, but Jesus commanded those who stood by to take away the barrier that hindered the dead man from hearing.

Causing people to *hear* the gospel demands more than merely speaking gospel words. There's hardly a young person in North America who has not seen a Bible verse on a billboard, or Billy Graham on TV, or read "Jesus saves" legends on bumper stickers. That's the gospel in its simplest form. But many have never really heard that Jesus offers them life.

When you bring young people to camp, you find many ways to remove barriers of suspicion, ignorance, prejudice, and fear. You do this by living with campers in a true-to-life atmosphere for an extended time where they can witness the effects of the gospel on real people. Many times a day, the camper hears the gospel articulated, not in a church setting which may be alien to his usual life pattern; but in camp, where adventure, play, and an array of intriguing new experiences capture his interest. As a camp counselor you can literally roll away gravestones where spiritual death holds young campers. This is the privilege of Christian witnessing.

Jesus' second command at the graveside was directed to Lazarus, now four days dead. Sometimes Christians seem to believe that soul-winning is a human task. Not at all. We can only remove the stones through a clear witness so God can speak to the dead. This witness includes articulating the salvation formula, but it is far more! When a person finds life in Christ, it is completely the work of God. No friend of Lazarus dashed into the tomb to apply artificial respiration. Jesus cried, "Lazarus, come forth!" and he came. The story does not tell us *how* he came out of the tomb. We are told that he came out bound with grave wrappings; hands, feet, and head. God worked the miracle of new life for a man still enshrouded with graveclothes.

Then Jesus issued His third command to those who stood by. "Loose him and let him go." Maybe that's Christian education. Surely it is the ministry of the Christian camp, your ministry as a counselor. Your campers will not be perfect, and neither are you. But you are moving toward freedom, toward maturity, toward cleansing. We share the privilege of helping one another escape the shroud.

Helping campers discover freedom in Christ, is the aim of the counselor. Christian freedom is both theological and practical. Too often we major in theology, making everyday life seem almost incidental to the gospel. Yet the New Testament teaches that everyday life *is* the gospel, a life of love, joy, peace, patience, kindness, goodness,

The Heart of the Matter

faithfulness, gentleness, self-control. It is summed up in one word—Christlikeness.

Since everyone learns more from seeing than hearing, camp offers young people a week-long object lesson in the gospel, and you become the object. Don't allow yourself to hide behind the grand Christian alibi, "Don't look at me, look to Jesus." Unless counselors live Christlike lives, not much will happen in camp chapel.

AIMS FOR THE CAMP

Considering all the kids in the world, no Christian camp should operate at less than capacity. We have established the spiritual purposes of winning campers to Christ and leading them toward spiritual maturity. But having approved the definition, several specific aims should be adopted which you as a counselor can help achieve. Growth is one aim.

How big is too big? You can't determine that numerically. As long as the camper enjoys satisfying experience with spiritual results, total numbers are of little consequence. Given enough land, buildings, and leaders, there seems to be no practical limit to the number of campers that can be served each week.

Having established a practical maximum for your facilities, attendance becomes a vital factor. An empty cot is a lost opportunity, not to mention the difficulties caused for the camp treasurer. Many financial problems can be solved by simply filling all the beds with paying campers. A good counselor is the camp's most powerful promotional agent. Campers who have a bad week will not be back no matter how fetching the promotional movies or four-color brochures might be.

Many camps need to explore new territories for recruiting campers, and every counselor should be a recruiter. One small church set a goal of fifty campers for the next season, more than double the number registered from that church in any previous year. The pastor and people took up the challenge and talked camp all year. When the season approached and the quota had not quite been met, the people visited homes in the neighborhood, inviting children to camp. Since most Christian camps charge less than secular private camps, prospects were not hard to find. The quota was exceeded, and several children from neighborhood homes found Christ. Camp is a prime evangelistic opportunity.

A California Camp Opened

Another church opened its heart to an orphanage in Mexico, sponsoring children even though they spoke only Spanish. When other campers discovered that the orphans had no spending money, they pooled their funds to give each child a dollar. Then the orphans learned that the camp planned to take a missionary offering, and each one tithed his spending money to the project. When I talked with the leader, tears filled his eyes. Five of the orphans had found Christ. Reaching more campers means touching more hearts for the Master, and that's what Christian camping is all about.

Growth in program concepts is another aim for camps. Should each year be little more than a rerun of last year and the year before? Perhaps you can suggest new ac-

The Heart of the Matter

tivities. Some camps rent horses from nearby stables. One camp bought the season's leftover bicycles from a discount store and laid out a bike route on back roads. An Illinois camp sponsored a 300-mile trek for more adventurous bike riders, concluding at the camp. A camp leader in Canada built a string of Conestoga wagons. Many camps extended their programs into wilderness areas through canoe trips, horse pack and back pack trips or beach hikes. Now and then someone grumbles that all of this detracts from the "camp." Far from it! Adventurous programming reaches campers and shows that leaders are concerned more about spiritual goals than real estate.

Aims for Counselors

Ask any camp director what his greatest need is and he will reply, "Better counselors." I don't recall a single exception. Most camps need more money, and many desire more land. Construction never seems to end. But when camping comes down to the basic issue, better counselors looms as the greatest need.

Except for Sunday school teachers, camp counselors make up the largest single body of Christian lay workers. The growing number of salaried counselors, particularly head counselors, is a gratifying development in Christian camping; but the majority continue to be volunteers, and most of them serve for a one-week period.

Many have pointed out that a camper is exposed to more gospel influence in one week at camp than through regular church attendance the rest of the year. This in no way demeans the church, of which camp is but an extension. It merely points out the frightening responsibility assigned to

Christian camping in general and to the counselor in particular. The counselor spends more hours with the camper than other staff members combined!

The camp counselor is responsible to many people. First you are accountable to God who has entrusted into your hands for a week or more, a small group of campers. Betraying this trust through carelessness or neglect can result in great harm. As a counselor you are responsible to pastors and Sunday school teachers who share your concern for the camper's spiritual welfare. While churches do not own people, dedicated pastors care very much what happens in camp.

You are responsible to the camp director and to the camp sponsors. The efforts and investment of many people focus on your cabin where you largely determine whether camp succeeds or fails. And of course, you are responsible to parents who rely on you to care for their children. Making the rounds one evening, I paused near a cabin where it was obvious the counselor had stepped out. I heard the boys talking. One or two were building their egos by foul language and stories. Younger lads sharing this cabin were being exposed to thoughts alien to their parents' desires. The counselor, off on some trivial errand, lost an opportunity to send boys off to sleep with more wholesome thoughts in their hearts. Parents trust you to care for their children's minds, bodies, and souls.

The responsibility you feel will most keenly relate to your campers, that small band of people who share the cabin with you. What you are, some of them may become. That's a responsibility! The camper leaves behind his home and family and the distractions of a godless world. Several

The Heart of the Matter

times each day he focuses on spiritual matters: the Bible, prayer, God's claim on his person. Conditions in camp are ideal for the Holy Spirit to work. Yet with all these advantages, you as the counselor remain camping's greatest force for Christ. Young people accept a gospel that works, and camp provides the laboratory where faith can be demonstrated.

While you sharpen your camping skills, determine that you will keep on growing as God's person committed to a great assignment. Many years ago I coached a playground football team, a rugged bunch of athletes who averaged 83 pounds. I recalled from earlier years that football boils down to two fundamentals: blocking and tackling. Since I knew little about the fine points of the game, I concentrated on those two factors, and my team went undefeated through the season. We won all four games. If you want to be a winner, concentrate on the fundamentals.

The fundamentals for Christian growth are simple: the Bible and prayer. Too often Christians concentrate on trick plays or fancy formations, unaware that those who use these so effectively have mastered the fundamentals. Until you develop a meaningful personal devotional life, you can expect little spiritual strength. That should be your major personal goal.

Might I suggest a place to begin, if you have not found a satisfying pattern for personal devotions? Adopt one manageable scripture portion and live with it for a time. I will suggest several, but you may come upon others that meet your needs more fully. It doesn't matter too much where you begin, for the Lord uses the whole Bible as the textbook for living.

If you find memorizing a satisfying exercise, fine. But strive to master the *ideas* of your adopted portion rather than the precise words. And read many translations and versions. Read the portion several times a day, at least morning and night. Often a key verse or phrase will emerge with special richness.

Having read the portion until its ideas are familiar, discipline yourself to think through the principal ideas at idle moments through the day. You will find the words of your favorite version forming quiet background music for your thoughts. Remember Psalm 1:2? "In his law he meditates day and night." Writing the Bible passage on a card you can tuck in your purse or pocket will aid you in remembering it.

Two spiritual adventures will overtake you as you follow this program. You will be delighted with the insights you gain into God's Word, small things you missed in beloved passages. And you will be amazed how often your companion passage exactly meets an emergency in your inner life!

Early in this devotional exploration of one passage, you will discover a new dimension of prayer. You will find yourself talking the passage back to the Lord, thanking Him for promises, questioning about puzzling statements, claiming provisions for life. You'll find a new basis for prayer that will expand into frequent mental conversations with God about small things around you. The Bible then becomes God's Word in reality for you as you respond with your thoughts and feelings.

On the surface this approach might seem too limiting. The Bible is a large book with treasures on every page.

The Heart of the Matter

Can the Christian afford to linger for days or weeks in one chapter? Indeed he can, for such lingering creates a hunger that carries a person beyond that passage and results in more Bible reading than ever before! How long should you remain in one passage? Until you feel fully at home in it. You will feel gentle regret at taking up a new passage, like leaving an old friend. But when you do, the adventure begins all over again.

I have found this practice becomes true *personal* devotions, God speaking to me according to my needs day by day. Prayer grows to new richness, freed from the stiff, formal attitudes we somehow pick up from hearing public prayers. Frequent chats with the Lord whenever my mind is free from pressing matters sweeten each day.

Probably you will need to set a definite time for daily reading that fits your schedule. Any learning or growth program demands discipline. But the blessings from ten minutes in the morning will echo throughout the day and linger in your spirit as sleep overtakes you at night.

Here are several passages you might consider for in-depth devotions:

1 Corinthians 13	Psalm 37:1-9
Galatians 5:22-25	Joshua 1:1-9
2 Peter 1:3-11	John 15:1-11
Psalm 1	1 John 1:1-9

The list could be extended to include other choice passages. Many other equally fruitful approaches to personal devotions can be discovered, but try my suggestions for a time. You'll be delighted at the results.

You recognize, of course, that counseling demands spiritual maturity; and only as you grow in your total Christian life will you improve as a counselor. Camp brings the whole year into focus in one week of ministry, and all the preparation in the world won't help much if you reach camp a spiritually impoverished, defeated Christian.

Aim also at increasing your understanding of campers. Read books suggested in the bibliography, attend workshops where you can learn from others, participate in church leadership where you can observe young people, watch for magazine articles dealing with youth and their problems. Many frustrations counselors suffer, grow out of a failure to understand the nature and limitations of the age group they serve.

Build your personal counselor's file. Clip stories and ideas you can use next summer. Swap ideas with other counselors. Read many books on camping, jotting down usable ideas. Preserve your evaluation of each year's experience, the ideas that worked and those that didn't. Become the most proficient counselor you can, and as you master blocking and tackling, work out a few trick plays.

Refining Aims for the Camper

We have pointed out that evangelism is only the prelude to growth. Winning people is not enough, if by "winning" we settle for a momentary decision. Saving faith always leads to action, a lifelong search for the high purpose to which Christ calls men. Your aims for the camper include the challenge to excellence in all of life as befits a person who belongs to God.

Excellence in Faith

Sometimes Christian youth are accused of being shallow. If this is true, guilt must be shared by leaders who fail to recognize that young people respond to challenging leadership. As a counselor you must exhibit and teach the high standard of faith Paul expressed to Timothy: "Be thou an example of the believers." Lead your campers toward excellence through meaningful devotions and conversation. Acquaint them with Christ's deeper claims to full commitment; but don't expect young Christians to run, before they have learned to walk.

Excellence in Vocation

Challenge your campers to high adventure in vocation. Countless Christian leaders have heard God's call to service while in camp. God still seeks young people with willing hearts for missionary posts around the world. Avoid creating a tension between those committed to church-related vocations and those who are not, for God's call to the secular world is equally valid. But point campers toward professions and occupations where they can serve people. Help campers discover the dignity of their person, and challenge them to become their best wherever God may place them.

Excellence in Service

Urge your campers to enlist immediately in God's service in their church, at school, or through outreach ministries. Churches have often been too reluctant to use young people. The theory that teenagers can't effectively teach Sunday school has been exploded. Older youth can work with younger children in club programs. We are witnessing a spiritual youth movement unprecedented in modern times, when young people show a boldness for Christ unequaled by most adults. Remind campers that service includes the home. Many Christian young people are careless at home, reflecting ingratitude or indifference for the sacrifices parents make. Youth gladly enter the serious work of God's kingdom when they are challenged to excellence in service.

Excellence in Leadership

The counselor who succeeds best is the one who does the least. Can this be true? Yes, if you work at developing leadership among campers. More skill is required to work through your campers than to do a task yourself. Depending on the campers' age, utilize every opportunity to cultivate leadership skills. This doesn't suggest full self-determination for immature campers, but you will find opportunities for sharing leadership. When decision-making or planning needs arise, consider how your campers can share. Use them to plan and present devotions and outings. Skill in leadership comes through practice under guidance. Show campers how to lead, and do not do for them what they are capable of doing, even when their performance cannot match yours.

So this is the heart of the matter, focusing on our aims as servants of Christ through camping. Throughout history great Christian movements have degenerated into mere institutions, often impressive and enduring, but no

The Heart of the Matter

longer a soul-winning, life-changing force. Camping can lose its spiritual verve too, and in some places it has.

While we must never sacrifice excellence in facility and performance through indifference to quality, we must constantly call ourselves back to our declared goal, to fulfill God's purpose in the lives of people. And now we consider what is, in some respects, the most important day of the camp week.

STUDY GUIDE

1. What do you understand the following sentence to mean in your work as a counselor? "While we talk about evangelism and Christian education as separate concepts, they are in reality two inseparable aspects of God's plan."
2. "The grand Christian alibi, 'Don't look at me, look to Jesus.'" What does this mean to you as a counselor living with your campers?
3. How does numerical growth in camper registration relate to the aims of Christian camping?
4. How does growth in program concepts relate to the aims of camp?
5. The chapter names four areas of responsibility for counselors. What are they?
6. Describe the pattern for personal devotions given in the chapter, and list values you might find in following it.
7. List several ways you can grow in understanding and skill as a counselor.
8. What four areas of excellence should the counselor covet for his campers?

9

Well, They're Gone

ONE MORNING NEXT SUMMER you'll wake up and realize that camp is over. There were times you thought this day would never come, but it has, and you're both sad and glad. Campers are packing and rolling up sleeping bags. Buses and cars roll into the parking lot. Little brothers and sisters scurry about searching for the right camper. All that remains are good-byes, autographs on the camp photo and evaluations.

Evaluations preserve the value of camp, so don't treat them lightly. The week you planned so long and worked so hard to accomplish has ended. What really happened? An honest evaluation is not easy, but it is vital. Without evaluation and analysis, camps rarely grow; and campers seldom receive meaningful follow-up.

Not every camp supplies adequate guidelines for evaluation; but if yours does, follow them closely. You will be expected to evaluate your campers and probably your camp. I would suggest a third area—*self-evaluation*. This may prove the most difficult, but it may be the most important. Self-evaluation permits you to preserve your experiences of the week as a basis for a continuing, growing counseling ministry.

Evaluating Campers

We looked at factors related to camper decisions in chapter seven. We urged you to treat all decisions with dignity. Now you will measure the meaning of decisions as they affected the lives of campers. And you will relay information to the home church or other follow-up persons, so that the camper will be encouraged in his new commitment.

Data for your evaluation has been collecting all week in your memory and on scraps of paper, through interviews and from the observations of others. Specific decisions should be a matter of formal record, of course. Attitudes and responses throughout the week may be less formally noted. Achievements should not be overlooked. Any unusual problems or marks of growth should be noted. A sentence or two intepreting the camper from your viewpoint will prove most helpful. Prepare three copies: one for the camp files, one for the follow-up persons at home, and one for your records. You will find this useful for personal follow-up. (See pp. 138-39 for a sample form.)

If you have done your job well, you will know your campers well and will have had opportunities to chat with each one privately. You will find a measure of affection for each one which will tempt you to gloss over certain kinds of information that may cause the camper problems at home. Be objective and honest! A negative report helps concerned persons at home build on your corrective work at camp.

Beware of the temptation to take the camper evaluation reports home under the guise of a more thorough job. Compel yourself to wrap up camp work at camp. The kind

CAMPER EVALUATION*

(to be completed by counselor at end of camp)

Dear Pastor _____:

Here's a report on _____.

He (She) attended Camp _____

from _____ to _____, 197____.

This status and progress report should help you better understand and guide him (her). Please pass this form on to his (her) Sunday School teacher. (If the camper doesn't attend Sunday School, we suggest that _____

_____.)

Counselor making report _____

_____ Date _____

Camper's street address _____

City _____ State _____ Phone _____

Age _____ Grade (this fall) _____ Sex _____ Race _____

	Yes	No
Did assigned Bible work	____	____
Reads Bible on his own	____	____
Tells others about the Lord	____	____
Growing in faith	____	____
Athletically inclined	____	____
Used to being away from home	____	____
Critical, fault-finding	____	____
Easily discouraged	____	____

Well, They're Gone

    Tries to domineer   ___ ___
    Sense of inferiority   ___ ___

Stronger qualities _____

Weaker qualities _____

Main interests _____

Physical disabilities or health problems (if any) _____

_____

Skills developed during camp _____

_____

Swimming classification: Advanced ☐   Intermediate ☐
         Beginner ☐   Nonswimmer ☐

Spiritual decision(s) made at camp (what and when) _____

_____

Apparent results of my personal counseling _____

_____

My opinion of camper's present spiritual status _____

_____

(Any additional comments on back of this sheet.)

_____
_____
_____
_____

*Used by permission of Scripture Press, Wheaton, Illinois.

of person who gives a week to camp rarely goes home to idleness.

Do not hesitate to consult with other staff members in evaluating your campers. Provide as well-rounded a picture as possible of each camper, including those matters which might reflect on your skill. You are not likely to reach every camper equally well.

The Final Touch

It is always in order for you to personally follow up your campers. Camps vary so much in relation to their constituency that it is difficult to suggest one follow-up pattern. Denominational camps usually draw campers and leaders from a group of churches which maintain relatively close contact through the year, and it is assumed that these churches view the camp as an extension of their Christian education ministry and will care for the campers they send.

Agency camps often have a formal relationship with the club or society in the camper's home area to which camper follow-up is assigned. But private Christian camps may draw campers from many areas with no single follow-up pattern possible. Here the camp must look after its campers or they will be left to drift.

Form letters represent the minimal kind of follow-up. A form letter can scarcely be more than minimal—nice to get but hardly exciting. Often such letters come as Christmas greetings. The best follow-up is a personal note from the counselor relating some meaningful incident from camp. This demands discipline of time and purpose, as well as some form of records to sort out the campers as they merge in memory over the weeks. It would seem tragic if a camper made a decision for Christ, and no one cared enough to let him know he remembers.

Some counselors employ a simple rest-hour exercise to remind the camper of camp. Each camper is provided a paper, envelope, and stamp. One rest hour is devoted to writing a letter—to himself. Campers are asked to tell themselves what camp meant to them, what decisions were made, what adventures were enjoyed. The letters are sealed and handed to the counselor, who drops them in the mailbox in midwinter.

I recall a letter like that. An immigrant boy and his dad from Czechoslovakia had been given temporary lodging in the church, and we succeeded in sending the boy to camp. Shortly after camp the father and son left, and we wondered often if their short stay had left an impact. About Christmastime the letter arrived, addressed to Peter. We did not know the forwarding address. I opened the letter and read, "Yesterday I accept Jesus as my Saviour. I am glad."

You may wish to drop a note to a camper's pastor or parents, telling of your encounters through the week. You will exercise good judgment, of course. A note to a home unsympathetic with the purposes of camp could do much harm. A letter directly to the camper will accomplish most.

Prayer remains your constant follow-up privilege. Some campers you will never forget. Others you must add to your prayer list as a reminder. As you pray, your ministry continues. Perhaps someday the Holy Spirit will nudge you to pick up the phone and call a lad working in a filling station. You have no idea what such a call can mean.

Evaluating the Camp

Wise camp directors seek evaluations from as many reliable sources as possible and from varying vantage points. You hold the key view of camp, for you see how the overall program affects the camper. Again, sheer honesty is demanded. Your candid opinion of high and low points in the week, along with your thoughts as to why a program feature failed, will help greatly in planning camps to come. The final test of any program element is this: Did it help achieve the camp's objectives in the camper?

You may detect personnel or facility needs. Ask yourself, "What made my work difficult, or easy?" Did the daily schedule flow smoothly with a minimum of abrasive circumstances? At what point in the day or week did camper interest sag? When did you feel uncomfortable in leadership? How might camp be enriched through new features or facilities? Was adequate provision made for your personal needs?

A key question for evaluation is this: What precamp information did you find lacking that hindered adequate preparation? How could the camp more adequately prepare you for counseling?

You may be encouraged to recommend improvements in the camp. Program specialists will not view camp as you do, so give careful thought to the program as you discover campers relating to it. Since camp is for the camper, put yourself in his place and seek ways camp could become more meaningful. The recommendations from counselors provide vital data for camp planners.

Self-Evaluation

Well, how did you do? That's the most difficult evaluation of all. For one thing, we have been urged not to credit self with success. That is unhumble. Everyone wants to do better. Granted. But *did* you do better? Before any evaluation can be made, one must establish criteria for measurement.

Sometimes in my itinerant life I come upon pastors wallowing in the mire of despair. All light is darkness and joy is gall. It's easy to say, "Cheer up, brother! It can't be all that bad." But it is. On man's usual scale of achievement, the poor fellow is absolute zero. What then? I try to provide a new point of reference, one not subject to the whim of cranky deacons or perverse church members. The true index for measuring success is one's standing with God. The man who walks with God can't be defeated.

I can't claim great success for this remedy for the pastoral blues, but the truth abides nonetheless. We can't control circumstances, and we can't all win the cleanest cabin award the greatest number of times; but God has provided the potential for walking with Himself. Paul experienced shipwrecks but did not count them defeat.

You were a success if your walk with the Lord became more vital. You can't measure success by the number of prizes your campers won, for you may have had superior or inferior campers. Your success can be discovered only as time goes on, perhaps decades later when the fruit appears from seeds planted by your godly life and consistent love for a camper. Beware of pride in your "decision" box score! Decisions mean many things. Has your concern for campers increased? Do you love God's Word more dearly? Does the time of prayer mean more to you? Are you more keenly aware of your shortcomings? These are the criteria for spiritual success.

Early in this book, I suggested that you take up residence in Romans 12 as a good place to learn how to be a good counselor. Now I would urge you to live for a while in Philippians 3 as the place of self-evaluation. I know there are mysteries here, but there is a clearly defined goal. As we establish goals, we can measure progress.

As Paul evaluates his personal assets, he places them in perspective as to their worth, rejecting what man ordinarily considers to be virtues, for the surpassing worth of knowing Christ Jesus. Then Paul takes us deeply into his self-awareness. When you have mastered Philippians 3:10-11, you will be well on your way toward success as a Christian leader. And you will understand Paul's mature humility in the following verses. That goal Paul mentions in verse 14, and the prize, what might they be? Try reading it this way. It satisfies me. "I press toward the goal for the prize: the upward call of God in Christ Jesus." For life on earth, the prize is the calling! If during your week at camp you felt the tug of the Spirit to give yourself in service to help others Godward, you had a good week.

I have included a self-examination in this chapter. Don't write this off as a spiritualized escape from honest evaluation. You will want to check up on your grasp of the counseling machinery, and your growth in specific skills. You will note the moments when frustration or anger caused you to fail momentarily. But you will forgive yourself, with the knowledge that, being a mortal, such moments

Well, They're Gone

will likely occur again. Only as you grow spiritually can you strengthen your counseling role. You may not feel content, but press on! Paul had been working at it a good deal longer than you when he wrote Philippians 3.

TWENTY QUESTIONS FOR COUNSELORS

Be specific and honest! If you recognize no progress in an area, admit it. And don't accept perfunctory Bible reading and prayer as meaningful devotions, nor mere civility as Christian grace.

Be candid, then forgiving! Only as you look honestly at yourself can you grow. This may be a mental exercise only, but greater value is gained if you write your responses. You will not be expected to share your discoveries, but you may uncover pockets of personal need for special prayer.

1. Has my week at camp enriched my personal devotional life?
2. What significant Bible truth did I gain from Bible reading this week?
3. What new prayer burdens were impressed on my heart?
4. Did I maintain my personal devotional life through the week?
5. What counseling interviews did I initiate with my campers?
6. What counseling interviews were initiated by my campers with me?
7. How thoroughly did I prepare for cabin Bible study and devotions?
8. When did I lose my composure with campers or staff?

9. Which of my campers did I seem to reach most effectively? Least effectively?
10. What made the difference in my effectiveness?
11. Which new skills or crafts did I explore this week?
12. What new ideas did I conserve for next year?
13. What points of tension developed in my relations with the camp progam?
14. What specific plans have I made for camper follow-up?
15. How accurate and thorough were my camper evaluations?
16. When did I indulge my self-interests rather than serve my campers?
17. When did I initiate action beyond my normal duties?
18. What needs that I could have met did I pass by because they were not my duty?
19. What plans have I made to improve my counseling skills?
20. What specific names and needs have I added to my prayer list?

Next Year and Beyond

I met a little lady in her 70s a few years ago, whose eyes lit up like Christmas when she learned I was a camper. She retreated immediately to her room and returned with a bundle of neatly wrapped packages. Each one contained samples of campcraft, some showing many years' use. This lady had been a handcraft leader in camps for thirty years, and she was all worked up over the coming season. She had discovered several new handwork ideas, and she couldn't wait to share them.

Well, They're Gone

She had been a housewife and mother, but camp was her annual assignment from the Lord. Her scrapbooks and bundles of crafts bore testimony of a ministry worthy of a saint. She never aspired to become the evangelist or director. Her skill was in handcraft and in loving and enjoying campers. I wondered how many thousands of lives were different because of this little lady.

Perhaps the Lord is appointing you to a life of camp counseling. I expect camps will continue as long as the Lord delays his coming. And many of them will depend on volunteer counselors like you. These camps deserve the finest leadership possible; and that means experienced, growing leadership. Why not preserve your experiences through a notebook and file system? Good ideas are all around, and the mind easily loses what at the moment seems unforgettable. Counseling becomes exciting when you think of it not as a chore but as a ministry.

I have alluded to the importance of books. Sources for Further Information lists helpful books in several categories of camp activities and includes annotated bibliographies. These can guide you to many hours of worthwhile study. As you cultivate your personal spiritual growth, work on the skills of leading people and on new activities to create interest among campers. As you read, feed ideas into your notebook.

Growth comes through association with people as well as through reading. No doubt you serve the Lord in your church as a Sunday school teacher, youth worker, or club leader. Training in these areas will strengthen you in camp work as well. Workshops, seminars, and discussion groups where you share with other leaders, stimulate new ideas and provide for growth.

In many areas Christian camp leaders meet regularly for fellowship and sharing. Christian Camping International unites camp leaders around the world, sponsoring national, regional, and sectional conferences. You will find much help here.

Your camp may offer advanced training. Christian schools sometimes conduct classes for Christian education workers with sections for camp leaders. Magazines carry articles of value to campers. Be alert for opportunities to grow. Camp counseling is a vital ministry.

Concluding the writing of a book is nearly as hard as closing off a sermon. So much more needs to be said. But many sermons fail because they try to say everything and leave nothing for the mind to figure out and apply. Obviously, *Camping Guideposts* does not treat camp counseling exhaustively. And it boasts no scholarly pretense. Hopefully, these pages have stimulated your thinking and possibly generated a resolve. If this has happened, my goals are realized; for your strength as a camp counselor lies within you—your dedicated spirit and God's Holy Spirit.

Happy camping!

Appendix 1

A WORD TO CAMP DIRECTORS

WHILE COMPLETING WORK on *Camping Guideposts*, I attended the fifth biennial global convention of Christian Camping International, attended by more than nine hundred delegates representing sixteen nations. An air of excitement prevailed, which promises a bright future for Christian camping. This was reinforced by the number of college students and graduates I met who were planning careers in camping.

A gratifying number of camp directors told me that they used *Camping Guideposts* as basic counselor training, making the preparation of this new book the more rewarding.

Many cabin counselors will be young people themselves, and I covet for them the delight of a life of Christian camping. A growing number of Christian schools are adding camping courses to their Christian education curriculum. State and federal legislation may compel camps to add professional leadership to qualify for continued operation. Above all, the mounting recognition of camping within the Christian community calls for more specially-trained leaders.

The best way I know to recruit professional camp leaders is to provide rewarding camp experiences for potential candidates. This calls for careful training to equip young counselors for satisfying work. The study guide which follows each chapter has built-in devices for adaptation to individual camps. Blending these studies with your own counselor training program can prove highly effective. If your camp has not developed a counselor training system as yet, *Camping Guideposts* provides a place to begin.

RECRUITING COUNSELORS

The question of where to get good counselors plagues all camp directors. If your budget permits a salaried staff, the problem is partly solved; but the vexing matter of screening applicants remains. I have indicated throughout these chapters that attitude and commitment to Christ are more important than leadership talent, but these qualities are not so readily determined.

I have designed several questions in the chapter study guides to reveal how trainees see their task. You must determine standards for performance and procedures for evaluation and let counselors know that their work is under scrutiny.

What age should a counselor be? Once we were told that high schoolers were too young, that they lacked the maturity and dedication required to lead children. Some said that young campers respond more favorably to adults. (An adult was presumed to be anyone over twenty-one.) Both of these viewpoints have been discarded as careless generalizations. High school youths can lead juniors effectively, while many persons over twenty-one are totally

Appendix 1: A Word to Camp Directors

unsuitable. Children respond to love and maturity regardless of the age of the counselor. And don't overlook the older person as a prospective counselor.

Every camp must cultivate its camper and leader constituency and build traditions that aid in recruiting the right kind of people. *Camping Guideposts* is aimed particularly at the camp which uses volunteer leaders, usually for a one-week period. Such persons often lack formal training in camp work. Your prospective counselors should be required to read this or another book you feel is suited to your camp philosophy. Tackling a counseling assignment without some preparation is perilous indeed.

These concluding pages contain resources for leadership growth. The book list is suggestive rather than comprehensive, books I feel will prove helpful to counselors. In the long run, effective counseling grows out of the creative spirit of the counselor as he matches action to opportunities. The finest tools in the hands of a poor workman don't count for much, but a jackknife in the hand of a craftsman accomplishes amazing artistry. Your task as a camp director demands close attention to the spirit as well as the mind and muscles of your counselors.

Appendix 2

CAMPING ASSOCIATIONS

Christian Camping International
Box 400
Somonauk, Illinois 60552

Membership open to camps, individuals, and students. Sponsors sectional, regional, and international conventions. Publishes the *Journal of Christian Camping*, a bi-monthly magazine.

American Camping Association
Bradford Woods
Martinsville, Indiana 46151

Membership open to camps and individuals. Sponsors sectional, regional, and national conventions. Publishes *Camping Magazine* monthly.

Sources for Further Information

Because prices fluctuate so frequently, those listed here may not remain accurate. Also, old titles pass out of print, but most of the books listed below seem secure in their usefulness and should be available for years to come. You can purchase them at, or order them through, your local bookstore.

The selected listings that follow have been adapted from the *Annotated Bibliography of Camping* compiled by S. W. Smith and E. Towns, published by Christian Camping International. I would recommend that every serious student of camping secure this book along with Barbara Ellen Joy's *Annotated Bibliography on Camping*, Burgess Publishing Company. Several of the books listed below contain helpful bibliographies.

Administration and Organization

Blueprint for Quality. Ted Johnson and Lee Kingsley. Chicago: Harvest, 1969. Pp. 180. $1.95. A valuable handbook for every person involved in administration of a Christ-centered camp; provides basic guidelines for camp organization, facilities, procedure, staffing, safety, purchasing, and promotion.

Camping: Administration, Counseling, Programming. J. Shivers. New York: Appleton-Century-Crofts, 1970. $7.95.

LEADERSHIP AND COUNSELING

Are the Counselors Prepared? Marie Hartwig and Bettye Myers. Minneapolis: Burgess. $2.50. Designed to acquaint camp counselors with problems they may expect to face in dealing with children.

The Camp Counselor's Book. Edited by Mary L. Northway and Barry G. Lowes. Minneapolis: Burgess, 1963. $3.00. Paper.

Camp Counselor's Manual. John A. Ledlie and Francis W. Holbein. New York: Assn Press, $1.75. A camp counselor's daily job, his qualifications, relationships to campers and directors. Section on record keeping. Paper.

Counselor's How-to Book. Scripture Press. Pp. 48. $.75. Clearly spells out the opportunities, duties, and qualifications of a Christian camp counselor.

Creative Counseling for Christian Camps. Joy Mackay. Scripture Press. Pp. 128. $1.50. Gives proven answers to your biggest problem: counselor training. Covers all phases of camping from outdoor cooking, first aid, craft, sports, storytelling, to setting spiritual goals, dealing with campers' problems, and winning and training them for Christ.

Help! I'm a Camp Counselor. Norman Wright. Gospel Light. $.95. Easy reading, yet packed with practical hints for counselors in any Christian camp. Paper.

If the Counselors Really Know Them. Marie Hartwig and Bettye Myers. Minneapolis: Burgess. $2.50. Designed to acquaint camp counselors with problems they may expect to face in dealing with children.

The Leader and Creativity. I. W. Weschler. New York: Assn Press. Order from National Council of Young Men's Christian Association, New York. $2.00.

So the Counselors Are Puzzled. Marie Hartwig and Bettye Myers. Minneapolis: Burgess. $2.50. Designed to acquaint

Sources for Further Information

counselors with problems they may expect to face in dealing with children. Paper.

These Are Your Children. Gladys Gardner Jenkins, Helen S. Schacter, and William W. Bauer. Third edition. Glenview, Ill.: Scott, Foresman, 1966. $11.25.

CHURCH CAMPING: SPIRITUAL EMPHASIS

Camping Together as Christians. John and Ruth Ensign. Richmond, Va.: Knox. $1.50. A leaders' guide for three major program emphases: Christian stewardship, Christian growth, and Christian community, with suggested procedures for planning the program and training the leaders.

Junior Devotions for Campers. Ken Taylor. Wheaton: Tyndale. $1.50. Action photos and life-related devotional readings for junior-age boys and girls at camp, based on Bible texts from the Living New Testament. Paper.

Teen-age Devotions for Campers. Ken Taylor. Wheaton: Tyndale. $1.50. Daily devotional readings and memorable photos for teen campers, with texts from the Living New Testament. Paper.

CAMPING OUT, WOODLORE, AND CONSERVATION ACTIVITIES

Audubon Nature Bulletins. New York: National Audubon Soc. Set $5.95. Bulletins are 8½-by-11 inches, four to six pages covering sixty-five subjects in a nontechnical fashion under seven categories: weather, trees, soil; flannel board stories on conservation; nature crafts; quiz games; plant identification; insects and spiders; and animals and how they live.

Backpack Cookery. Hunter's Encyclopedia staff. New York: Collier. $.95. Paper.

The Boy's Book of Backyard Camping. Allan A. Macfarlan. Harrisburg, Pa.: Stackpole, 1968. $4.50. At-home ways with shelters, tents, camp cooking, knot-tying, direction-finding, outdoor games. For grades five and up.

Camping and Camp Cookery. Hunter's Encyclopedia staff. New York: Collier. $.95.

Camping Manual. Edited by Fred Sturges. Harrisburg, Pa.: Stackpole, 1967. $3.95. Paper with spiral binding.

Cookout Book. Helen E. and Philip S. Brown. Los Angeles: Ritchie Ward. $2.75.

Golden Guide to Camping. Robert E. Smallman. New York: Golden, 1965. $1.00.

Golden Nature Guides series. New York: Golden. $3.95 and $1.00. Pocket-size guides to various areas of the natural world. Over one hundred full-color pictures in each. Titles: *Birds, Flowers, Insects, Stars, Trees, Fishes, Mammals, Reptiles and Amphibians, Seashores, Weather, Rocks and Minerals, Zoology, Photography,* and *Sailing.*

Handbook of Trail and Wilderness Camping. John A. Ledlie. New York: Assn Press, 1970. $1.00.

Inspiration Under the Sky. Dorothy Pease. New York: Abingdon, 1963. $2.00.

Weather Science Study Kit. Order from Superintendent of Documents, Washington, D.C. $1.00. Includes booklets, maps, and loose sheets of information.

Nature-Oriented Activities

Collect, Print and Paint from Nature. John Hawkinson. Order from American Camping Association (see Appendix 2). $2.95. Author shows step-by-step how to print and paint by using plants and natural objects with readily available art materials.

Fun with Naturecraft. Avery Nagle and Joseph Leeming. Order from National Recreation and Park Association, Washington, D.C. $4.75. Simple projects using nuts, feathers, cones, leaves, flowers, twigs, etc.

A Leader's Guide to Nature-Oriented Activities. Betty van der Smissen and Oswald H. Goering. Ames, Iowa: Iowa State U., 1968. $3.95. A handbook for community leaders of youth and adult hobby groups. Gives advice in crafts, games, hiking, trailing, outdoor cookery, day camping, and outings. Includes nature photography, the study of birds, stars, animals, gardening, rocks, and minerals.

Learning About Nature Through Crafts. Virginia Musselman. Harrisburg, Pa.: Stackpole. $3.95. One hundred fifty simple, just-for-fun, and useful things children can make from nature's storehouse, plus ready-to-use suggestions for hours of rewarding child-adult sharing of ideas and achievement. Complete and easy-to-follow directions for projects.

Learning About Nature Through Games. Virginia Musselman. Harrisburg, Pa.: Stackpole. $3.95. More than three hundred active and pencil-and-paper games that stimulate questions and supply answers. Learn-as-you-play fun.

Stargazing. Janet Nichelsburg. Nashville: Church Recreation Department, Southern Baptist Sunday School Board. $3.85. A group leader's guide with a nontechnical approach to teaching campers basic facts about astronomy.

Teaching in the Outdoors. Donald and William Hammerman. Minneapolis: Burgess, 1964. Pp. 120. $2.95. A valuable resource; deals with the rationale underlying outdoor education; the relationship of learning in the out-of-doors to the school curriculum; effective techniques and procedures for outdoor teaching.

Group Activities

Active Games and Contests. Richard J. Donnelly, William G. Helms, and Elmer D. Mitchell. Third edition. New York: Ronald, 1958. Pp. 672. $8.00. Covers the entire scope of active play. Planned for all play directors; acquaints the user with all types of play activities of an active nature, and offers selections to fit almost any occasion that might arise. Over two thousand games and contests are covered. Illustrated.

The Boy's Book of Rainy Day Doings. Allan A. Macfarlan. Harrisburg, Pa.: Stackpole. $4.50. Almost two hundred games, puzzles, contests, and handcraft activities.

838 Ways to Amuse a Child. June Johnson. New York: Macmillan, 1970. $.95. Illustrated idea book offering children from six to twelve years hundreds of things to make, to do, and to learn.

End of Your Stunt Hunt. Helen and Larry Eisenberg. Nashville: Church Recreation Department, Southern Baptist Sunday School Board. $.50.

Indian Crafts and Lore. W. Ben Hunt. Order from National Recreation and Park Association, Washington, D. C. $2.95. Contains hundreds of exciting Indian activities and crafts for boys and girls. Complete directions given for making warbonnets, beadwork decorations, peace pipes, totem poles, and many other objects.

Let's Play a Story. Elizabeth Allstram. Nashville: Church Recreation Department, Southern Baptist Sunday School Board. $2.75. Deals with creative dramatics for kindergarten children through junior high: story dramatization, pantomime, choral speaking, etc.

Let's Sing Together. Order from American Camping Association (see Appendix 2). Pp. 96. $.35. Songbook.

Omnibus of Fun. Helen and Larry Eisenberg. Order from American Camping Association (see Appendix 2). $7.95. An antidote for the dull moment, filled with thousands of "instant activities."

Program Activities for Camps. Harriet J. Berger. Second edition. Minneapolis: Burgess, 1969. $5.00.

Sources for Further Information

Rainy Day Fun for Kids. Claire Cox. New York: Assn Press. $3.95.

Sing. Edited by American Camping Association (see Appendix 2). Cooperative Recreation Service. Pp. 95. $.50. Songs of all ethnic groups. Fast songs, rounds, campfire songs, and inspirational songs.

Singing Youth. Compiled by John Peterson and the Singspiration staff. Grand Rapids: Singspiration. $1.75. Offers more than three hundred songs and hymns selected to mold church leaders of tomorrow.

Skit Hits. Helen and Larry Eisenberg. Nashville: Church Recreation Department, Southern Baptist Sunday School Board. $.75.

SHORT STORIES

Agents 13. Ruth I. Johnson. Chicago: Moody, 1960. Pp. 127. $.60. Stories of Christians with courage.

Agents 14. Ruth I. Johnson. Chicago: Moody, 1968. Pp. 128. $.60. Stories of Christians with courage.

Forty Stories for You to Tell. Gladys Mary Talbot. Chicago: Moody, 1952. Pp. 192. $1.95.

Jungle Doctor's Fables and *Jungle Doctor* series. Paul White. Chicago: Moody, 1971. Pp. 128 in each. $.60 each.

Nature Stories for Children. Vera Hutchcroft. Grand Rapids: Baker. $1.50.

Rat-Catcher's Son and Other Stories. Carolyn London. Chicago: Moody, 1971. Pp. 128. $.60. Missionary stories from Africa.

Stories I Love to Tell. Gladys Mary Talbot. Chicago: Moody, 1949. Pp. 156. $1.50.